DR BOB WOODWARD w... United Kingdom. Ha... schools, he became a c... in Thornbury, a centre based on the teachings ... ...y. He remained within the ...ment, living with and teaching childre... ...ith special educational needs, for some forty years, retiring in 2012. He took a special interest in understanding autism in children and young people.

At the age of 46, Bob received an MEd degree from Bristol University, followed by an MPhil at the age of 50 and a PhD from the University of the West of England at the age of 64. As well as being a qualified educator, he is a spiritual healer and the author of several books. He has been married for some 46 years and has five grown-up children and currently ten grandchildren.

By the same author:

Spirit Healing (2004)
Spirit Communications (2007)
Spiritual Healing with Children with Special Needs (2007)
Trusting in Spirit – The Challenge (2018)
Knowledge of Spirit Worlds and Life After Death (2020)
Journeying into Spirit Worlds (2022)
Karma in Human Life (2022)

Autism – A Holistic Approach (with Dr Marga Hogenboom)
(3rd edition 2013)

MEETING SPIRIT BEINGS

How to Converse with Personal Guides,
Guardian Angels and the Christ

Dr Bob Woodward

CLAIRVIEW

*The author encourages readers to make their own choices and decisions
in relation to the contents of this book. Any advice, recommendations
or teachings given herein should be subject to individual judgement.*

Clairview Books Ltd.,
Russet, Sandy Lane,
West Hoathly,
W. Sussex RH19 4QQ

www.clairviewbooks.com

Published by Clairview Books 2024

© Bob Woodward 2024

This book is copyright under the Berne Convention. All rights reserved. Apart
from any fair dealing for the purpose of private study, research, criticism or
review, no part of this publication may be reproduced, stored in a retrieval
system, or transmitted in any form or by any means, electronic, electrical,
chemical, mechanical, optical, photocopying, recording or otherwise, without
the prior written permission of the copyright owner. Inquiries should be
addressed to the Publishers

The right of Bob Woodward to be identified as the author of this work has
been asserted by him in accordance with sections 77 and 78 of the Copyright,
Designs and Patents Act, 1988

A CIP catalogue record for this book is available from the British Library

ISBN 978 1 912992 57 7

Cover by Morgan Creative
Typeset by Symbiosys Technologies, Visakhapatnam, India
Printed and bound by 4Edge Ltd, Essex

Contents

Acknowledgements

I wish to send my heartfelt thanks to everyone who has contributed to this book: Michael Allen for transforming my handwritten manuscripts into clear type and to Viktoria Szente for arranging these into a unified format. To Anne Lewis and Michael Luxford for writing the Foreword and Afterword respectively. My Editor at Clairview Books for his continued interest in and active support of my various research inquiries. Last but not least, to all my friends across the threshold who have so willingly responded to my initiative to enter into conversations with them. Only through this cooperative effort in fully conscious communication, can this new book now be offered to a wide readership. Many thanks once again.

Preface

The purpose of this book is to share with readers how we can begin to awaken our connection with certain beings across the threshold. It is this threshold of consciousness which separates our everyday sense world from the supersensible world of spirit beings.

The book is arranged in three thematic parts, each of which was originally a separate research enquiry. However, my Editor's idea to unite these enquiries in one volume was, I think, a moment of genuine inspiration! This is borne out by the natural transitions from Part I to Part II, culminating in Part III. The 'red thread' of awakening conscious connections with those who dwell in spirit, is transparently clear.

To a large extent, the text consists of lively conversations, enabling readers to have easy access to the contents. Not only is our thinking called upon in these chapters, but also our feelings and will are engaged through the inherent invitation and challenge to find our own ways to connect with friends in spirit. In this sense, the book may well serve as an awakener for our own insights and intuitions.

I very much hope that what is offered in these pages can become a real source of inspiration, reassurance and encouragement to all who, like me, are walking along their own paths on their unique spiritual journeys.

There is no doubt that in the troubled times we live in, which includes serious existential threats to our core humanity, there is an urgent need for us to awaken to a wholesome, and inclusive, spirituality. This spirituality encompasses connecting with our spirit guides, guardian angels and the cosmic Christ Being. But, having free will, the initiative for such contacts is very much on us to ask for, in order to receive.

All blessings, Bob
Advent 2023

Foreword

I am honoured to be writing this Foreword for Bob, having known him since 2004 when he first asked me for a reading. My name is Anne Lewis and I am a spiritual healer and medium. I have been working with spirit guides and healers intentionally for over 30 years. Ever since I was a state registered nurse and registered paediatric nurse, I am positive that spirit has been working with me and guiding me, although I had not started my spiritual training at the time.

I first trained as a spiritual healer and, through sitting in development circles over a few years, spirit awakened the other spiritual gifts of communication: a mixture of clairaudience, clairsentience and telepathy.

When Bob contacted me, I had never met anyone with such clear telepathy from their spirit guides. It was the perfect method for him, as he is a learned person with the gift of presentation in an almost scientific way. You could say we were the opposite in character and spiritual gifts. Despite this, the information we both received was the same, but shared in a very different way, with love and humour.

When you seek to learn from spirit, books are a good way of widening your knowledge. I used to read many books, but I found the personality of the authors coloured their writings. There was not one that stood out as exceptional.

This latest book of Bob's is, I feel, the culmination of his and spirit's work, written by spirit with Bob's clear and unbiased cooperation. This book would be the start of many people's journey to working with their spirit friends and guides. If only this book had been available when I was starting out on my journey, it would have helped in so many ways to give me more faith and courage in my own abilities.

The way Bob's guides finish each chapter, giving their own truth and understanding, feeds the soul. There is perfect harmony between Bob and his guides' input, so you know by reading this book that you are learning the truth about communicating with spirit in clear concise chapters, that leave you eagerly turning the next page. Welcome to the start of your journey of communicating with spirit.

Anne Lewis Min. ICSP

PART I

HOW TO COMMUNICATE
WITH SPIRIT GUIDES

Introduction to Part I

My purpose in writing Part I of this book is to share something of my own experiences in learning to communicate with those who live in spirit worlds. Why? By doing so, whatever I can share here may perhaps be of help and encouragement to others. By others I mean those people who do harbour a genuine wish to be able to strike up a *conscious* rapport with their friends in spirit. I emphasize the word 'conscious' because from the start it has been that 'awake' state of mind that has characterised my own methodology.

Since 2005, I have been on a spiritual journey of discovery in regard to communicating and cooperating with certain friends in spirit.* Now, from the outset, some readers may question the validity and truth of my journey. I welcome such a reaction. It is, I think, much better to be initially sceptical about such things than to be naive and gullible. After all, even assuming that the author of this book is sincere, honest and genuine in his account, this does not of itself guarantee that he is not misguided. While he may have convinced himself of his own abilities to engage in conversations with those across the threshold (between the sensory and supersensible worlds), we cannot simply believe or just accept what he says, can we?

Since the sixteenth century, we have lived increasingly in what may be called the 'scientific age'. This encourages us to carefully observe and think for ourselves, not just to blindly believe or have faith. Particularly of things or beings which are unseen! Well, as the author of this book, I couldn't agree more with this scientific point of view. I am certainly

---

*The guides who have contributed to this book are: Joshua Isaiah. In a former life he was a rabbi; Dr John. In a former life he was a medical doctor; Red Cloud. In a former life, he was a chief of the Sioux Native Americans; Raja Lampa. In a former life he was a Tibetan Lama; Markos. In a former life he was a Greek monk and philosopher; Pierre. In a former life in France, he was a Knight Templar; Isobel. She was my pupil in a former lifetime in India, when I was then a guru; Gopi Ananda. Likewise, she was also associated with me in a former lifetime in India.

not asking anyone to simply accept on faith what I shall write about in the chapters that follow. Neither do I ask anyone to simply believe the 'conversations' that I claim to have had with my various spirit guides, as published in the books prior to this new volume. Nor indeed to the 'teachings' also given in those books by allegedly discarnate entities. However, what I would certainly like to assume is that the readers of those earlier books, and of this one, are very willing to exercise an open mind, free from prejudices and preconceived ideas. To ask this is in no way to restrict any person's capacity for strong critical thinking and considered reflection. Indeed, both these inner attributes are, I feel, essential in order to arrive at an informed and sound point of view. So, with these cautionary words, I hope to have set the tone with which we may together proceed to explore the main theme of this project, namely, how to communicate with spirit guides.

In the chapters that follow, I will describe as clearly as I can the different factors which belong to my own inner methodology for such communications. In any serious enquiry or research project, it is essential to detail the particular methodology which has been used to obtain certain results.

I will also invite my guides to contribute their thoughts on these sub-themes. I do, of course, realize that each person will need to find their own way of engaging with those in spirit worlds. Whereas my way is telepathy with clear thoughts, others may have more success with receiving pictures and images, or perhaps certain feelings and sensations. We can also speak of having clairvoyance, clairaudience and clairsentience when referring to inner pictures, inner hearing or inner sensations. I can only describe in this book what, through experience and time, has become a reality for me.

This reality – which I did not expect or anticipate – of being able to communicate with 'spirit guides', began in 2005. As a process of learning and development, it is clearly described in my book *Spirit Communications*, published in 2007. I would therefore recommend interested readers to study that small volume. However, in brief, I can mention here that it was my initiative to write to Anne Lewis, a spiritual medium living in Yorkshire, that set the ball rolling!

I first contacted Anne in late December 2004, in order to ask her to give me a 'postal reading'. For this purpose, I sent her a letter with several questions, and also a passport-sized photo of myself, as she had requested.

My main reason for asking for a reading was to gain, hopefully, confirmation about my abilities as a spiritual healer. When I received Anne's reply in January 2005, the confirmation I sought was immediately evident in the picture of the spirit doctor who was then working with me, as presented to Anne's clairvoyant vision. This was very reassuring. I asked Anne for further readings and, in the third of these, the same spirit doctor, whom I know as Dr John, suggested that I could begin to link up with him directly, rather than rely on the services of the medium (i.e., Anne).* I took this suggestion of his as both an opportunity and a challenge. This then was the beginning of the path that I have been walking along for the past 18 years. In the course of that time, I have had contact and communication with nine spirit guides (as discarnate human beings), but also with some other friends, including my guardian angel and the nature god, Pan. Whilst it has in a sense become second nature for me to be able to readily converse with such beings, we will now proceed to delineate essential elements for the successful achievement of clear communications. I will begin each short chapter with commentary and then invite my guides to contribute to that particular theme.

---

*Woodward, *Spirit Communications* (2007), p. 29.

Intentionality

Without any doubt, our intentionality for wanting to communicate with those in spirit is crucial. In fact, I would say that it is crucial for *any* serious spiritual work. We need to ask ourselves, in all honesty, why we want to acquire this ability. What really motivates us? What is our reason, or reasons, for going along this particular path? Is it no more than idle curiosity perhaps, or could it be to do with our own secret vanity to appear rather special in the eyes of others? Might this ability even give us some sort of power or influence, setting us apart from less-gifted mortals? Isn't there a certain fascination associated with those who have the gift of mediumship and who can apparently talk with the dead?

Well, none of the above possible reasons constitute, to my mind, any true or legitimate reason for engaging in spirit communications. In fact, quite the opposite! Nonetheless, it is very important in the first place to become as clear as we can as to what our intentions really are.

To be of service to others *is* a worthy intentionality, as is our wish to help to move the world forward along a positive path – a path in which love for humanity, regardless of race, gender, religious affiliations or any particular 'isms', is the central motivating aspiration and striving. If we can examine ourselves inwardly and know that our motives are for the highest good for all, and do this with due humility, then we are indeed on the right track. This doesn't mean of course that we are saints rather than sinners! We can recognize our weaknesses and faults, but just because of this, we then aspire to develop ourselves to the best of our ability on the spiritual pathway that we choose to follow.

So, when we have satisfied ourselves that our intentionality for linking with friends in spirit is indeed sound, then we may begin to feel confident that, with the grace of God, we can achieve our aim.

Let me now ask Joshua, my main spirit guide, if he or another of the guides would like to contribute on this theme.

Bob: Joshua, can you give me a reply to this question, please?
Joshua: Shalom, my friend. Yes, of course I will. I would like to make a contribution on the matter of 'intentionality'.

Bob: Please do so.

Joshua. Well, my friend, what you have written above we are in agreement with. There is no doubt, as you have said, that it is indeed essential for anyone who wishes to link up with friends in spirit consciously to be very clear about their motives for doing so.

As you rightly say, it is necessary to look at ourselves very honestly in this regard, and not to fool ourselves into believing that our motives are genuine when in fact they are not! No, scrupulous honesty and self-knowledge is required to come to a just conclusion on this point. Now, we do not say that a person needs to have attained the 'mountain of morality', so to speak, in order to embark on this journey. None of us are saints, as you point out. Nonetheless, we do need to be clear, very clear, about the reasons for wanting to do this work. On our side of life, we must also have this clarity. Therefore, we will never impose ourselves upon you, Bob, or upon others on your side of life who wish to follow this path, this spiritual path. It should be done in all freedom and in full knowledge of what is required. Above all, that requirement is to serve 'the good of all'. That is really the most important thing, and with this I think I have made the contribution which I wish to make. All blessings, Joshua Isaiah.

Bob: Well, thank you, Joshua. I think we can draw this chapter to a close and turn our attention to the next theme, namely, 'Silence'. However, I will just add that our intentionality comes into play on each and every occasion when we link with those in spirit. Therefore, it is an ongoing challenge, and something we need to be mindful of.

Silence

As I mentioned above, in the third reading which I received from Anne Lewis, my spirit doctor, Dr John, communicated the following to me:

> I hope I have answered your questions to a satisfactory degree, and I wonder whether you would feel, as I feel, that if we could meet in the silence, where you could begin to feel my presence, that this would be a more satisfactory way of communication than meeting through a medium, albeit a medium who is walking under the guidance of the healing master.
>
> I am more than willing to come to you when you ask to sit in the silence, so that we can begin, or should I say continue our relationship, because by blending together in the silence, it helps when we do our healing work.*

As I said before, I took Dr John's words both as an opportunity and a challenge, and began to try to practise 'sitting in the silence', as he had suggested. This meant not only coming into a quiet place free of outer distractions, but much more importantly, trying to create such a space and time of silence within myself.

Anyone who has attempted to become inwardly quiet will know that this is much easier said than achieved! Our minds are often very busy places, filled with thoughts, images, memories, worries, concerns and demands for present or future actions. It requires some practice and discipline to gradually be able to enter into the silence. This is also a listening place and a state of mind. Here we can be more receptive and sensitive to what may come towards us. Now, having said this, my communicating with Dr John, and then also others, was very much on the level of mental thought-telepathy, rather than feeling any 'presences'. I will discuss this further in the next chapter. However, the ability to become silent and to listen inwardly is a prerequisite, I would say, for this telepathic process to take place.

---

*Woodward (2007), p. 29.

Becoming inwardly still and quiet was actually not new for me. I had been a daily meditant for almost 24 years, before receiving Dr John's invitation in 2005. My meditation always begins by first entering into the silence as far as I can. So, I had had a good deal of practice at acquiring this inner skill. As such, it would certainly be an advantage for anyone who is serious about conscious communication with their guides, to also take up some form of regular meditation. There are a variety of meditation techniques described in books on the subject, as well as a range of contents suitable for meditating upon.

Actually, it is not now necessary for me to sit in the silence, since I can communicate with my guides, if I wish to, when going for a walk in the countryside, or wherever. But, when I first began to follow up on Dr John's suggestion, I did very deliberately, intentionally, sit down quietly in my room in order to try to tune in with him. I think this tuning in is similar to when we have a real conversation with someone in daily life. If your mind is too busy, too full of ideas buzzing about, then you can't really listen to what the other person is saying. You need to bring yourself into a quiet, silent state of mind in order to follow your friend's train of thought, as well as being open to their expressed feelings or emotions. Perhaps, even sensing what lies behind the words themselves. For spirit communications to take place, I need to be able to enter the silence at will, though readers should not imagine this as lasting a long time. It can be seconds rather than many minutes. It is the quality of this activity, this state of consciousness, rather than its duration, which is important. So, at this point, I would like to invite a guide to contribute.

Bob: Joshua, I wonder if Dr John would like to comment on this theme?
Joshua: Shalom, my friend. Yes, John is happy to come in here.
Bob: Right, thank you, Dr John.
John: Yes, my friend, it is many years ago that I first made that suggestion to you to 'sit in the silence', and it has proved its worth. Your ability to communicate with us has come on in leaps and bounds since that time. As you have said, to sit in the silence is a prerequisite for receiving communications from spirit, because only then has one put oneself into that receptive state of mind. Of course, in our case, the mode of communication was to be by thoughts, because of your particular constitution. Perhaps for another person it would be more in the way

of images, as it is for Anne for instance, or for someone else, more in the feeling realm. Whatever mode is most appropriate for a particular person, the main point is that becoming still and inwardly quiet provides the space into which impressions can flow. Therefore, we would say that silence is indeed a quality which enables us to make ourselves known, one way or another, to the person on the physical plane who wishes to have a rapport with us in spirit.

We do not say that it is essential to become *completely* quiet or silent inwardly, since this would be a tall order for most people to be able to fulfil. No, it is rather the attempt to enter into the state of receptivity that is required. When we see that this is taking place, then we can make our presence felt to that person, again one way or another.

In your case, my friend, it takes the form of your awareness of our thoughts. So, with this I think I will bring my contribution to an end. All blessings, John.

Bob: Many thanks.

*

In the next chapter we will turn to 'thinking', which is, as far as I am concerned, the faculty that is paramount when I am engaged in conscious communication with those in spirit worlds. I will add that the state of silence and inward receptivity alluded to in this chapter can perhaps be well pictured in the demeanour of the heads or figures of the Buddha – which we can have in our homes – with their expression of inward contemplation with eyes closed and the ears exceptionally long, emphasizing a capacity for inner listening. This is an apt image of 'sitting in the silence'.

Thinking

As I have coined it, my mode for communicating with friends in spirit is 'mental telepathy'. What do I mean by this? I refer here to being able to receive the thoughts transmitted by those in spirit worlds. But how do we know that these are *their* thoughts rather than our own? Herein lies the challenge: to learn to distinguish when we are thinking to when someone else is *thinking in us*.

My initial clue that this was the way to go was provided for me again by Dr John in the fourth reading that I received from Anne Lewis. I had asked what sort of communication this would be when I made time to sit in the silence to tune in with Dr John.

Anne wrote:

> He says that, as you are a mentally active person, you will be able to access this area for communication, and you will be able to hear his voice in your head. Do not be impatient with this, because his thoughts will be in your voice, not his. You will have to be aware of your thoughts to determine which are his words and which are yours. To help you do this, when you sit in the quiet, he will give you a gentle peacefulness in the room where you sit. You will know when you recognize this, he will be about and will respond to your questions by thought. He himself is a more mentally-orientated person and as such, your communications will be mainly by clairaudience. This is the most accurate way of communication, he says, and he tells you to keep trying until you are confident that it is not all in your head.*

By 'not all in your head' he was indicating the distinction that needs to be made between one's own thoughts and the thoughts coming from another entity, in this case from Dr John. This indication was actually particularly pertinent for me because, ever since I was a child, I wondered where my thoughts came from. This inner

---

* Woodward (2007), p. 32.

13

questioning belonged, I think, to my naturally introverted nature. We know that some people are definitely 'thinkers' rather than 'doers' or 'feelers', if I can put it like that. And some, like me, are introverts rather than extroverts. According to my mother, I kept myself to myself as a young boy and was something of a 'closed book' and a loner. This description was also borne out by the first words of my Leaving Report from the Steiner school which I had attended from age 11 to 18, namely:

> Robert entered seven years ago as a boy who was thoughtful and withdrawn, appearing to be shy in contact with other people.

Now, the only reason that I include these personal remarks is to show that they do have a certain relevance now, many years later, in terms of my modality for spirit communications. Being a thinker, spirit found that clear thoughts were the best way of getting their messages across to me. Perhaps this will likewise apply to some of the readers of this book?

When I become quiet and take the initiative to ask those in spirit to give me counsel and advice or to respond to specific questions, then I do receive a clear flow of thoughts. This is, of course, an inner experience, although I can also verbalize it just as it happens, if I choose to do so. So, for me, this is the way in which communicating takes place. I do not see images, nor do I feel different sorts of sensations or 'presences'. Rather, I allow the thinking of the other to live in me. If I choose to, I can then also record in writing what I am receiving from my spirit guides or from others in spirit. Whilst I have often thought that it would be very helpful to also see my guides, from their point of view this is not necessary for me to be a good, effective channel for what they wish to convey. Therefore, we could say, clairaudience takes precedence over clairvoyance. And, as I have said, the essential skill to learn for mental telepathy is to be able to clearly distinguish who is thinking the thoughts that enter my mind. This is now a good moment to invite one of my guides to comment on this theme.

Bob: Joshua, do you know who would like to step forward to make a contribution?
Joshua: Shalom, my friend. Yes, Red Cloud would like to do this now.

Bob: Thank you. Over to you, Red Cloud.

Red Cloud: Thank you, my friend. Yes, the theme of this chapter is certainly one of the central ones for your way of communicating with us, as of course you are doing right now! As you have pointed out, it is the ability to distinguish where the thoughts are coming from that is the essential skill to be learnt. For some people who wish to communicate with us in spirit, this will come about far more naturally and easily than for others. Those of a more introverted frame of mind, and who are used to surveying their own thoughts, are more likely to be able to develop the capacity to perceive the flow of thoughts from another source. However, having said that, we must emphazise most strongly that a person must never allow themselves to be dictated to by thoughts from another. In other words, they must not lose or give up their own power or autonomy. This is really most important, because the last thing that we would wish to happen is that a person living in the body allows him or herself to become like a puppet on a string. You understand what we mean? To not allow themselves to become subservient in any way to beings outside themselves. This would be a dangerous – or at least potentially dangerous – situation for them to be in. There are beings who could manipulate or overshadow a human being in a way that would not be at all helpful. It could even lead the person to lose faith or trust in their own thinking ability, and this would then be the very opposite of what should happen. So, my friend, you see it is necessary to point to potential pitfalls when engaging in this form of communication. It is very important that a person is of sound mind and makes every effort to maintain that balance. Provided that is done, then mental telepathy provides an excellent means for us to communicate with those on your side of life.

We felt that it was important to bring through these cautionary words, a sort of warning if you will, so that anyone attempting to communicate in this way is forearmed, so to speak. We do not wish to scare anyone off from learning to use these inner skills, but rather that they take sensible precautions to ensure that the communications and contacts are sound. Remember, whatever is done should be done out of the right intentionality, in order to attract those on our side of life who are working also for the greatest good. All blessings, Red Cloud.

Bob: Well, thank you, Red Cloud. You have brought through important aspects of this work, which I might not have thought of myself for this chapter. Many thanks.

*

In the light of what Red Cloud has said here, the next chapter, with the theme of 'Trusting', is especially apposite, as we shall see.

Trusting

Before launching into this important theme, let me make the following observation. For the sake of clarity, the themes that are the subject of these various chapters have been treated separately. In doing so, I have attempted to analyse and identify different factors that belong to my way of engaging in spirit communications. However, it should be clear that in actually doing such communicating, all these elements belong together. They are integrated in, and integral to, the actual process. If I use a rather mundane analogy, I could compare learning to communicate with learning to drive a car. Just as it is necessary for a learner driver to come to terms with the accelerator, clutch, brakes, steering wheel, indicators, mirrors etc., so it is necessary to recognize the various elements involved in these forms of communication. As the novice driver proceeds through their lessons, in what was initially a new and challenging endeavour – namely to coordinate the different parts of the vehicle to produce a smooth journey – this is eventually achieved. The same is true in the sphere of spirit communications by integrating all the factors, which for clarity and transparency I have dealt with separately here. It is important to keep this fact well in mind, so that what has gone before, and what we shall be discussing now and later, are seen as forming a totality and wholeness.

So, to 'trusting'. Whenever we enter into conversation with others, I think we would hope for this to be based on an attitude of trust. At least, if it is to be a friendly, open and constructive discussion. Of course, if we are engaging in a controversial or very heated debate, mutual trust may be at a low premium. However, when we are concerned to establish communications with spirit guides, learning to trust ourselves and them is essential. In my book *Spirit Communications* (2007), I described in detail the process that I went through in making conscious links with my friends in spirit. Interestingly enough, one of the chapters in this book was entitled 'A Doubting Thomas'. Here, I shared frankly some of my own doubts, for example, of my ability as a spiritual healer. I also wrote about the earliest attempts that I made to receive communications from the other side. The chapter ended by emphasizing the need to develop trust, and I will quote from it here:

> However, there is no doubt that in working consciously with spirit, 'trust' is a key word and a key faculty which needs to be developed and strengthened. Trust and confidence allow things to take place which otherwise are obstructed and stifled by distrust and doubts.

A little further on I added:

> There is, however, a difference between 'blind' faith and trust, and faith and trust which gradually arises through experience, humility and insight. In the words from Joshua out of the eighth reading, 'Trust comes from the heart; it has nothing to do with the mental level…'*

Certainly, for me, building up trust in myself and in the reality of my spirit guides has been an ongoing process. This is, I feel, probably inevitable for anyone who is at pains to be honest with themselves and does not intend to indulge in wishful thinking or fantasies. In other words, for anyone who is serious about the path of spirituality they are following. I deliberately say 'spirituality' in order to take account of the many different paths that may be taken up, just as there are various ways to meditate. One size does not fit all, but rather each person needs to discover what rings true for themselves. However, the inner attitude of trust can indeed be common ground within this diversity of ways.

Perhaps for many people, and I include myself here, the main issue is to be able to trust *oneself*. To trust the veracity of one's experiences. It is probably much easier to extend trust towards others who you regard as being much further along the spiritual road than we are ourselves. There is, I suspect, a deeply human wish to find the guru, the master, the spiritual teacher in whom we can put our trust and who can tell us what to do. This may then give us a strong sense of certainty and reassurance.

It is, however, much more challenging and unsettling to think for oneself and to learn to rely upon one's own inner spiritual experiences. In actual fact, a genuine spiritual teacher or guru would, I believe, encour-

---

* Woodward (2007), p. 59.

age just this independent approach. Such a teacher as the late Rudolf Steiner (1861-1925), for example, did not seek unthinking followers or disciples, but rather those who were willing to tread the path themselves and carefully test out their own experiences. Exploration, not indoctrination, is the best way forward. Likewise, the Buddha exhorted his pupils not simply to believe what he said, but rather to seek for the truth themselves.

Therefore, the question of trust is first and foremost directed to each of us. Of course, to then also establish a trusting relationship to one's spirit guides is important. Since true guides always respect the autonomy and free will of their incarnate contacts, our trust will also strengthen as we get to know each other well. This is completely comparable to forming a good friendship with someone in earthly life. Trust grows ever stronger as the friendship deepens over time. Needless to say, distrust, on the other hand, widens the gulf between us and undermines true friendship. At this point, I will ask if a guide would like to contribute to our theme.

Bob: Joshua, would someone like to step forward for this?

Joshua: Shalom, my friend. Yes, Markos is here and keen to make a contribution.

Bob: Thank you. Please do, Markos.

Markos: Yes, my friend, thank you for letting me speak on this theme of trust and trusting. Now of course, as you have already eloquently said, to learn to extend trust is absolutely fundamental to working with your spirit guides. It is fundamental because it really provides the ground under our feet, so to speak. It gives the sure basis for the relationship between a person living in the body and his or her guides living in spirit worlds, for them to be able to relate in a healthy and wholesome way. Without trust, nothing of any value can be achieved. In your case, my friend, we know how long it has taken to establish this trust between us, mainly because of your own self-doubts. This is not of course meant as a criticism, but rather as an illustration of how the building up of trust takes time. It is not something that just happens overnight, but rather, requires work and dedication. Given a sincere and earnest approach to establishing a good rapport with us in spirit, we see how the trusting relationship grows on both sides of the veil.

It is far better that this trust grows steadily over time, than it being rushed and remaining unreliable. So, we would say to anyone who is seriously seeking contact and communication with the guides, that the gradual establishment of trust is an essential ingredient in this endeavour. Nonetheless, we also urge seekers to use their sound common sense and their own intuitive feelings, in order to feel happy with the relationships they are building.

Discrimination, in the sense of being able to have reliance on trust in your spirit contacts, is also important. As the saying goes, 'Fools rush in where angels fear to tread'. This means that you should test the waters for yourself and be as sure as you can that those you relate to are indeed trustworthy. In saying this, we do not wish to scare anyone away from establishing contacts with those on our side of life, but only to say that care is needed in all such undertakings. All blessings, Markos.

Bob: Right, Markos, thank you for that.

Again, as with previous contributions, what has been brought to us now by Markos leads directly into our next theme, namely, 'Identities'.

Identities

Who's who? This is the essential question of this chapter. Or, to put it another way, 'How do we find out who are our spirit guides?' This is clearly an important step towards developing a trusting relationship with our friends in spirit.

Let us first think of ordinary daily life and how we identify someone. This could be someone whom we know already, or it could be when meeting a complete stranger. In the case of someone we know, we will recognize and remember their physical appearance, and hopefully also their name. As we grow older, names can become much more elusive, though the person's face is often instantly recognizable, provided not too much time has passed since we last met. This situation can sometimes lead to some embarrassment as we struggle to put a name to a face.

With strangers, we don't have that same problem, since we usually exchange names when first introduced by someone else, or by introducing ourselves. The challenge, however, remains to remember this for our next meeting. When in conversations we refer to someone, be it a member of our family or friends, we usually refer to them by name rather than by giving any physical description. The latter might be required, however, if our friend's name doesn't register with whoever we are currently speaking with. So, we try to picture the person as clearly as we can and convey this description to our listener.

Another means of identification could be by recognizing someone's voice, their distinctive timbre and way of speaking. This is especially relevant when talking on the telephone. Yet other tell-tale clues can be had by recognizing the particular stance, movements and gestures of a person at a distance from us. How they walk is very individual. So, in a variety of ways, we can usually confirm for ourselves another person's identity and exactly who they are. How does all this stand when we're concerned now with our spirit guides?

Well, as with the examples given above, there may be various means of identification. Inner sight, sound, feelings or sensations, may provide the certainty we seek. For example, a good friend of mine who was clairvoyant was often able to see my two main guides, Dr John and Joshua, standing on either side of me. We had something of a standing joke as to which of these guides was taller or shorter according to my friend's vision.

As I am not clairvoyant, I have had to rely on getting the names of my guides. Sometimes these names have first been given to me through other people. For example, via Anne Lewis, my medium friend, I first received the names of Dr John and Joshua Isaiah. The book *Spirit Communications* contains the initial conversations I had with both of these guides. Dr John usually addressed me by name (Bob) when coming through to me, whereas Joshua began with the greeting 'Shalom'. Another of my guides, Markos, was first introduced to me by the psychic artist Peter John, whom I had met at a local 'Mind Body Spirit' fair. The name of my guardian angel, 'Philip', I learnt from another medium many years ago. So, in this way, via others, I received these first introductions. However, with all of my other guides, including Red Cloud, Raja Lampa, Pierre, Isobel and Gopi Ananda, the names came to me inwardly, into my conscious mind. If I want to ask a question to any particular guide, I address myself to them by their name. On the other hand, if I am engaged in writing, I can first ask Joshua which of the guides wishes to come through. Alternatively, I can simply be receptive to the name that comes clearly into my mind.

So, for me, it comes back to practising mental telepathy and getting their names when I am communicating with my guides. As I mentioned before, I have often wished to be able to see them too, but so far, this has not been the case for me. Nonetheless, through practice and experience over the years, I have come to rely on the way things work for me and for them. Moreover, since communication always takes place through my initiative, I will direct my specific query to one or the other of my guides to get the ball rolling, so to speak. Then, through my conscious receptivity and inner listening, I can also be aware of the name of any other guide that chooses to step forward.

Clearly, I can only share with you how that is for me. This may well be different from my friends Peter John and Anne Lewis, as also for yourself. Each person will need to discover how to begin to consistently identify their own guides. From my own experience, I have sometimes recommended that someone simply asks for the name of the guide to be given, whether inwardly or through some other channel. I do feel that knowing the names of your guides gives a very personal connection and link. If you happen to have, or gain, clairvoyance as well, then all to the good! I think we have once more reached the point when some input from my guides will be helpful.

Bob: Joshua, who can help us with this theme, please?

Joshua: Shalom, my friend. Pierre would like to come in here.

Bob: Thank you, please do so.

Pierre: Yes, my friend, let us consider the question of how best to identify your guides. By 'your', of course, I refer to those who are reading this book. You have already made clear your own way of doing this. We would advise that whoever is seeking for contact and communication keeps an open mind about how their guide or guides will identify themselves. You can rest assured that guides will do everything they can from their side of life to come through in a way that makes their identity as clear as they can to their earthly contact. You realize how important it is for there to be transparency about knowing who is coming through. Indeed, there is nothing worse than confusion and vagueness in this enterprise. Just as in your ordinary daily lives it is essential to know who you are dealing with, so it is when establishing connections with us in spirit worlds. Therefore, the guides will use every means available to them to make their contacts understand and recognize who exactly is coming through from spirit. Depending on the sensitivities and abilities of their friends on earth, they will find the best means of establishing that link and identity. More than this we cannot say, because it very much depends on each individual case, on the circumstances and opportunities available in each instance.

However, the main thing is to rest assured that guides will do their best to make clear who they are in their relationship to that earthly contact. All blessings, Pierre.

Bob: Right, thank you, Pierre. As you say, every person would just need to be open to the efforts of the guides in this matter. However, once the link has been made, then dialogue and conversations can begin. We shall turn to this theme of dialogue next.

Conversations

As I described above, the guide who first made himself known to me, via Anne Lewis in 2005, was Dr John. This was directly in response to my questions about my abilities as a spiritual healer. Dr John was the one who was working with and through me when I was doing healing sessions.

However, in the fourth reading, which I received from Anne in April 2005, she and I were introduced to another of my guides, Joshua Isaiah. Actually, his name was only then revealed in the sixth reading, two months later. Joshua's role in spirit was and is different from Dr John's, in that he is there for teaching, learning and spiritual development. Having made my conscious links with these two guides, I was in a position to ask them various questions. Naturally, with Dr John the questions centred around the healing work, whereas with Joshua they could be more diverse. This was then the beginning of entering into dialogues and conversations with my two main guides. These fascinating exchanges are available to read in my first book, *Spirit Communications*.

It is important to emphasize the conversational character of such contact with the guides, because this is a mutual enterprise. If we were only to be the recipients of teachings or advice, it would only be a one-way traffic! Certainly, for quite a while it was my practice to write down these conversations with the guides in my notebooks. However, in the course of time, I also got used to simply conversing with them in other settings. In particular, I enjoyed to do this whilst out in the local countryside. This was a 'freeing up', one could say, from writing down these exchanges to talking together whenever the spirit moved me. That is to say, when I had particular questions to ask, and sought counsel and advice from Dr John or Joshua, or perhaps both of them.

As the years passed, the time eventually came when I felt the impulse to write another book concerning my work with spirit guides. I would say that it was as soon as I had this fresh impulse that I started to become aware of other guides. In fact, it is true to say that precisely because I intended to write the second book that certain guides then made themselves known to me. The book entitled *Trusting in Spirit—The Challenge* was published in 2018 and written ten years later than *Spirit Communications*. I would like to recommend interested readers to also peruse this volume. The format for the chapters was to receive teachings from the guides and then to follow up with conversations on those particular contents.

I have adopted a similar format in my more recent publications, with the conversational style being an essential feature. In fact, in this way I often challenge the guides about what they have said, in order to gain greater clarity and understanding. This seems to be totally acceptable to them, and I feel that this is a good thing. It is not helpful to be overawed or subservient in any way to what any guide has to say to us. Yes, by all means respect and be grateful for teachings or advice received, but nevertheless be prepared to actively question and even challenge this. Thereby, we enter into true, lively conversations and cooperation with our friends in spirit worlds. I think that genuine guides do welcome these sorts of challenges, rather than expect us to feel somehow intimidated by their spirit presences. Whatever we do together should be in a spirit of friendship and mutual cooperation for the good of all concerned, including, of course, for the readers of our books.

Let me now ask if a guide wishes to contribute to this chapter.

Bob: Joshua, can you tell me if one of my guides wishes to step forward?
Joshua: Shalom, my friend. Yes, Isobel is keen to come forward for this.
Bob: Right, thank you, Isobel.
Isobel: Yes, my friend, let me say the following. Conversation is absolutely essential in communications with you. It puts us on an equal footing, and this is an important part of taking responsibility for our relationship. I say this because it would not be a healthy state of affairs if a person on your side of life felt that they must bow down in some way to us who live in spirit worlds. This is not at all what is wanted by us. No, we welcome a true cooperation between us, between those who live on the earth plane and those of us who live in higher dimensions of existence. Therefore, conversation is key to expressing a healthy and balanced interchange between us. This is why we have been keen to converse with you whenever you take the initiative to begin such a conversation. We deliberately do not

impose ourselves upon you, but rather wait for your request for help or guidance. This is the best way in which we, as guides, can be of service to those on the earth plane of life.

So, to sum up, my friend, we welcome conversation as an expression of the cooperation which respects your freedom to contact us in spirit when you wish to do so. And this way of doing things is something we would recommend for others to follow also. All good wishes, Isobel.

Bob: Thank you, Isobel. I think you have made things very clear by your remarks.

Now we can move on to our next theme, namely, 'Safeguards'.

Safeguards

Why do we need a chapter on this theme? Can't we just assume that any contacts we may have with those who live in spirit worlds is always going to be for the best, and therefore we can't really put a foot wrong? The short answer to that is no, we can't make that assumption. Instead, we need to be able to exercise our sound common sense and discretion and use our own moral compass.

This of course also relates back to when we spoke about 'identities'. It is also very much connected to our first theme, namely, 'intentionality'. Safeguards, then, *are* necessary so that we do not possibly end up demonstrating to our detriment the saying, 'Fools rush in where angels fear to tread'. Let us explore what sort of precautions we need to take when seriously seeking communications with those in spirit.

In the first place, we need to be very clear about our intentionality and our motivations for wanting to have contact. These motives should never be egotistical or selfish. Neither should they be to achieve any sort of power over others, or for personal fame or acclaim. No, the only true motivation must be to be of service for the greatest good for everyone involved, whether that then takes the form of receiving helpful counsel or teachings from our spirit friends, or perhaps to give some needed reassurances. We need to understand that according to our intentions for good or bad, we will attract corresponding entities towards us. If our intentions are good, then we can feel confident that only helpful beings will respond to us.

We also need to recognize that there do exist in spirit and soul worlds beings who wish to take advantage of ill-prepared human beings, and who can be manipulative and troublesome. We therefore need to be on our guard so that we do not just open ourselves to all and sundry. Yes, we want to practise receptivity and sensitivity to making spirit contacts, but only towards those guides and friends who have our best interests at heart. This would, of course, include our own guardian angels.

Ultimately, the very best safeguard is to do what we do out of love, because unconditional love is the most powerful force for good in the universe. This love also totally respects human freedom and free will. Remember, genuine guides will never impose themselves upon us, or seek to be coercive and influence us to do anything against our own choices. There is, we know, a certain human tendency, especially in spiritual strivings, to be quite willing to give up our own power to some exalted leader or guru. We want to be led along a path, and simply told what to do. This approach is, I think, fraught with dangers and alarm bells, and is not to be recommended. While it is no doubt good to have respect for those who have walked a spiritual path for many years, and in the process gained valuable knowledge and insights, this does not mean that we should give up our own power to them. Indeed, as I've said earlier, genuine teachers, gurus or initiates will not expect us to do this, at least not in modern times. Rather, they will help empower us to make our own experiences and to stand on our own two feet. We should also expect this same attitude towards us from those in spirit to whom we wish to link up with, consciously. I use the word 'consciously' very deliberately.

Although I am aware that some mediums enter into some degree of trance when contacting spirits, this has never appealed to me personally. I do acknowledge that so-called trance mediums may bring through information and insights of a high calibre. A case in point would be the various teachings of White Eagle, which were transmitted through the trance mediumship of Grace Cooke (1892-1979). According to a leaflet from the White Eagle Publishing Trust, she 'was quite unconscious of what White Eagle was saying as he used her vocal organs'.

There is also a tradition in shamanism of entering into such altered states of consciousness. While such practices may indeed lead to impressive inner experiences and teachings, again I am not myself inclined to these avenues. All my contacts with those in spirit have been made in full, waking consciousness. If anything, consciousness is heightened rather than lowered. I feel that this leaves me with the degree of inner freedom that I consider essential for such work, and my guides also respect this. So, in short, I would definitely recommend only seeking fully conscious communion with those in spirit worlds.

Of course, it is perhaps a fine line to tread between being inwardly receptive and open, but also being alert, aware and conscious. To that also belongs what we discussed earlier about identities and being able to identify who we are working with. Perhaps, in particular, to have a sense that we are in contact, genuinely, with the real person or being in spirit realms, rather than with some cast-off psychic part of that person. For example, Rudolf Steiner speaks of mediums sometimes communicating with the so-called astral (or soul) corpse or shell of a person who has died, rather than making a clear link with the spirit individuality *per se*.

How then would we know the difference between the psychic shell of a person and their own true being? Especially if we ourselves are neither experienced clairvoyants nor initiates? I don't feel qualified to give a full answer to this question. However, I would say that in building up our links with our guides, we will have a real sense of who we are speaking with and the quality of the communications we receive. These positive experiences can give us reassurances that we are indeed making genuine and wholesome connections. Again, I would emphasize our good intentionality, clear motivations and a loving attitude as the best of safeguards in all these endeavours.

Of course, and hopefully needless to say, we would never enter into such work whilst under the influence of alcohol, drugs or other mind-altering substances. We need to have the clearest possible consciousness, gained through our practices on our spiritual path, to have control over our own thoughts, emotions and deeds. It's not that we need to have a total or rigid control over our minds and emotions, but rather that we have ourselves well 'in hand', so to speak. Above all, that we exercise a balanced personality that is not given to wild extremes or flights of fantasy. 'Levelheadedness' would be an apt description. I suggest we now ask a guide to give us some input on our theme.

Bob: Joshua, can one of the guides help us to be clear on the theme of 'safeguards' please.
Joshua: Shalom, my friend. Yes indeed, Gopi Ananda would like to speak on this.
Bob: Right, thank you. Gopi, please enlighten us further.
Gopi: My friend, thank you for giving me this opportunity to come through and to give my views on this theme. In the first place, it is indeed essential to be very clear about why a person wishes to have contact with their friends and guides in spirit. This is the first safeguard, and in a sense the most important one. There can be no ambiguities here, but clear thinking is required. Of course, there may

be a variety of reasons for seeking such contact, such as help, advice, counsel, teachings, reassurances, etc., but whatever the particular reason may be, the mood and attitude of making contact is all-important. We cannot emphasize that enough. Idle curiosity, self-seeking agendas, and so on, are not sufficient reasons to establish such linkages.

You have covered these things well in what you have said already, my friend, and so we do not need to elaborate on this further. Safeguards are simply a way to ensure that the contacts which are made are trustworthy and sound, that they are of good quality and that all those involved are working for the greatest good of all. Provided all this is properly understood and applied, then people need have no fear about establishing such contacts. All will be well if the necessary precautions have been taken. So, with that being said, we would wish to encourage all those who are thus inclined to make efforts to contact the guides. These guides – and everyone on earth has their guides in spirit – look forward to being of greater help and assistance to their incarnate friends. It is just by two-way cooperation on both sides of the threshold that good supportive relationships can be forged. You know, my friend, from your own experience how helpful this can be. So, although safeguards should indeed be put in place, these should then enable all those who are sincere and serious in their strivings to make positive progress. We welcome such contacts and look forward to making ourselves known to our friends on the earth plane. After all, we as guides have also lived on earth in our incarnations, and know that we all now live in a time when fully conscious relationships between us and our human friends is of great importance. It enables a true cooperation to come about. And this, after all, is the goal which we all hope to achieve. All blessings, Gopi Ananda.

Bob: Thank you, Gopi, for your contribution. What you have brought will lead us quite naturally into the next theme of 'Cooperation.'

Cooperation

It was around 50 years ago that I first read a book entitled *Pioneering in Conscious and Cooperative Mediumship*. Not long afterwards, in my 20s, I met the author of this volume, Mrs Iris Ratsey, and over the years greatly valued her friendship and wisdom. She published the book in 1966 and describes therein how she was guided to establish conscious communications with friends in spirit. Interestingly, it was through having her own experience of the efficacy of spiritual healing that led on to, 'five years which were to be utilised as experiencing in esoteric methods of direct training, communication and service.'[*] These five years were then just the beginning of the process of inner development, clairvoyance and cooperation that Iris established with her guides and mentors in spirit. But above all else, what I remember about Iris was her dedication to 'service'. As she wrote, in reference to a good friend of hers:

> There are many such light-bearers in this country and all over the world. They work in their own Centres, usually helped by groups or teams of like-minded people, men and women of goodwill, who are gradually becoming known as the New Group of World Servers. Each group going about its work to aid God's plan for humanity quietly and without fuss. This method of working is particularly noticeable among the many healing centres in this country today, all of which is indicative of the future work of the Aquarian Age.[†]

Iris was also a healer, and I remember that on occasion I received some healing from her and Mrs Ellie Beevers, who, back in the 1960s, both lived in the Red House in Cheltenham. This was also, I believe, the headquarters of the movement for Universal World Harmony (UWH) that Iris served in. No doubt, a central part of that impulse was to help make people aware of the reality of spiritual dimensions

---

[*] Ratsey (1966), p. 20.
[†] Ratsey (1966), p. 21.

and in gaining a true understanding of our human, spiritual nature. A postal two-year course that they ran called 'The Quest' was designed with these aims in mind.

I have shared the above because it indicates the direction of service that belongs to the theme of 'cooperation'. Cooperation with our friends in spirit may take the form of active healing practices, receiving counsel or advice when we ask for it, or bringing through teachings and knowledge on a variety of subjects. For example, in gaining a knowledge of spirit worlds and of life after death; receiving guidance on inner development and journeying into spirit worlds; or perhaps gaining an understanding of the workings of karma in human life. In other words, by learning truly to cooperate with our guides and friends in spirit, we can aim to increase our knowledge in order to be of better service and help to our fellow human beings.

There are many aspects of such conscious working together across both sides of the threshold, between the earthly and spiritual dimensions. And it is not simply a matter of those on earth being the grateful recipients of what spirit beings can bestow on them. No, those same spirit beings, which include discarnate human souls, are also often in need of what *we* can give to them. For example, Rudolf Steiner gave definite indications and specific meditations for how those on earth could be of service to the so-called 'dead'. This service can include reading to them contents which contain definite spiritual substance and 'nourishment'. Some people do this particular form of communion on a regular basis.

The other side of this cooperation can be experienced in becoming more aware of the inspirations and helpful insights that flow to us from those same friends who are now living in spirit worlds. No doubt, a lot depends here on our sensitivities and awareness towards such interactions, but simply to know that our deceased loved ones are not far away is already a great support in life for many people.

Belonging to such cooperation would also be our acknowledgement of our own angel. As I understand it, our special guardian angel has been with us throughout all our incarnations. Therefore, we really do have an ever-present and ever-faithful friend in this spirit being. The usual way in which my own angel, Philip, greets me when he comes through to communicate is to say, 'My friend and brother'. There is, I feel, a lot in those words. To take completely seriously that each of us has an angel being at our side is quite something, is it not? How many people ever give a thought to this in the rush and tumble of daily life, with all its demands on our time and energy? And yet, would it not be a source of strength, of comfort and reassurance, to know that a being of light is with us continually? And how is that for our angel, if we effectively ignore him or her? If, instead, an awareness and conscious cooperation can gradually be established between this special friend and ourselves, then we might also be able to look at our own lives in a different light.

Well, this is but one important example of how cooperation can be of mutual help. The same can also be said of our spirit guides, in the sense that they are human beings who live on the other side of life. As I understand it, each of us has at least one such guide linked with us at any time. We will go further into this theme later on.

Whilst we have mainly looked at cooperation in terms of our own personal intentionality for consciously communicating with friends in spirit, we can also consider this in a much broader context. By this I mean when either individually, or in groups or teams, we are searching for real-life solutions to major world challenges and problems. The world is certainly not short of such challenges! Whether it is dealing with global warming and climate change, pandemics, drought or floods, disaster relief efforts, conflicts, etc., we could really use all the help we can get. If there really are spiritual worlds with beings of various kinds willing to help us when we take the initiative to ask for their help, I think it makes sense to do that.

In my book *Karma in Human Life*, there is a chapter devoted to 'Karma in Climate Change'. Herein, the nature god, Pan, speaks of his deep concern for the way in which human beings are mistreating the planet and her life forms. He speaks repeatedly of the need for cooperation between humans, himself, and the various nature spirits. In a Q and A session, I ask:

Bob: And will you, Pan, and your many subjects, work with us in cooperation if we recognize and turn to you?

Pan: We will, we will, we will. Even if you do not recognize us *per se*, if people do the right things, then we are working with you all the way.*

---

* Woodward (2022), p. 75.

This affirmation belongs to tackling a major world need. But we could retort that many religious people pray to their God, but what good does it do? Well, that's not such an easy question to answer, at least not in general. Individuals or groups may feel that their prayers are indeed answered. For some, however, the concept of 'God' may be just too big to grasp. So, perhaps starting closer to home by building a bridge to our guides and our angel may be much more doable? This is probably now the point where the input of an actual guide would be good to have.

Bob: Joshua, is there a guide who can help us regarding our theme of cooperation, please?
Joshua: Shalom, my friend. Yes, there is. Raja Lampa would love to step in here.
Bob: Right, thank you. Raja, over to you.
Raja: Yes, my friend, it is truly an important theme and chapter in your book, because much depends on this sort of cooperation in the times which you live in now. I mean by this that there is now a new spiritual awareness dawning, or wanting to emerge, which needs to be brought to the conscious light of day.

The problem is that daily pressures and the pressures of world events sometimes stand in the way of this new consciousness arising. Nonetheless, such an awareness is urgently needed, because without it, it really does appear as if the human race is entirely alone in the universe. However, the very opposite is the case. The spiritual worlds are much closer than most people think. In fact, you are all already living in them, but quite unconsciously. And therein lies the challenge: how to awaken yourselves to the reality in which you already live.

This is where cooperation has its part to play. Through truly cooperative endeavours, bridges are indeed built between the worlds and between the inhabitants of these worlds. When this is realized and acted upon, then humanity will start to realize what opportunities there are for mutual assistance and support. In other words, there is a very real resource at hand. It is just a question of being able to tap into it. Yes, just like you use your technology to link up with the World Wide Web, so you can use your consciousness to connect with the spirit beings who are around you. By doing this, you will be able to help find real solutions to some of your major problems, as well as receiving very personal and individual help when required.

Therefore, my friends, on behalf of the other guides, I would like to encourage you to grow spiritually and begin to practise the means by which your awareness and sensitivities can grow. Of course, we can only encourage you to move in this direction. The choice must be yours, since we cannot in any way interfere with your own free will. Nonetheless, let us take this opportunity to assure you that if you make the effort to connect with us, this effort will be reciprocated from our side of life. All blessings, Raja Lampa.

Bob: Thank you, Raja, for your input today. This book is intended to help us take up such opportunities.

Confirmations

You will recall from the Introduction that it was precisely because I was seeking confirmation of my abilities as a spiritual healer that I first wrote to Anne Lewis in December 2004. This led to me receiving the reading from her in January 2005, which in turn led to my introduction to Dr John, and then later also to Joshua Isaiah. These two remain as my main spirit guides.

In actual fact, I have again and again sought for confirmations of my work with these guides. On the one hand, this might be viewed as due to a lack of confidence in my own abilities, but on the other hand, I would say that it belongs to doing good research. That is to say, to actively seek confirmations of the validity of what one is doing. Let us therefore turn to this important theme and explore just what it includes and how we can go about it. Of course, as with all else in this book, I'm speaking from my own experiences, which may or may not be exactly applicable to you as the reader. That is for you to find out for yourself.

Confirmation regarding the identity of our guides is probably the one which first springs to mind. We want to know if we are right in this respect, because we feel that all else hinges on this being correct. Let us compare it to receiving some piece of information in daily life. In order to feel confident about its authenticity, we want to know where it comes from and from whom. 'Who told you that?', we might ask. Similarly, in receiving communications from alleged spirit guides, we want to know the identity of those guides. Perhaps we ourselves have first received the name or the appearance of such a guide. But how then can we be sure that we have this right? Well, in my own case, as already described, I received the names, and also, to an extent, the appearances of my two main guides – initially by Anne Lewis, the medium. In that sense, Anne had been the one to confirm to me that these guides were indeed closely linked and willing to work with me, each in their various ways. Thereafter began the process of my developing my mental telepathy, in order to clearly receive the thoughts as transmitted to me by John and Joshua.

This all took time and regular practice. It also required a definite strengthening of trust in my own abilities and in the reality of the guides as genuinely independent beings, not simply products of my own fantasy or wishful thinking. In my book *Spirit Communications*, you will read all about this journey of inner development. Indeed, the very fact that I dared to publish that book two years or so after my first introduction to these guides, is something of a testament, I would say, to my certainty of the validity of their identities.

In the same year as my book appeared in 2007, I met Neil Castleton, who, over the course of the following 12 years, became a very good and trusted friend. I think we met originally over a mutual love of crystals. Neil had a much greater knowledge of these wonders of nature than I did, and he utilized them in his therapeutic practice. So, it was in connection with crystals, and also healing, that our friendship first took off.

However, after a time, I also learned about Neil's clairvoyant abilities, his capacity to see auras, discarnate beings, guides, etc. Exactly when Neil first confirmed to me clairvoyantly the identity of Dr John and Joshua, I cannot now remember. But I certainly do recall clearly how, quite often when we met up, and at my request, Neil observed my auric field and would also see my two guides, one on either side of me. Again and again, he was able to confirm their presence. So, to sum up, both Anne and Neil confirmed the reality of my guides and this accorded with my own experiences of communicating with them telepathically. As of 2024, this has now been for some 19 years.

I think it likely that, like me, you also wish to seek for confirmations of the identities of your own guides. And again, like me, I feel confident that you will, one way or another, gain the very confirmations you seek. I must just add that, since 2016, the number of my own guides has increased from two to ten! Both Neil and Anne were largely able to again confirm for me their spirit reality through their clairvoyance.

Now, another essential aspect of this theme is in gaining confirmation of the actual reliability and credibility of any information that we receive from our spirit guides. We will therefore turn to this issue next. This was something which I also previously addressed in my book *Trusting in Spirit—The Challenge* (2018), in the chapter on methodology:

> I would say that if any information gained from spirit can be checked for accuracy, then it should be. Guides are not omniscient or infallible. Nonetheless, the advice and guidance that I have received for myself, and sometimes others, has proved to be very helpful, practical and reassuring. Real-life situations and circumstances are ever-changing and mobile and open to a variety of influences. Therefore, advice received at one point of time may differ from that which is most appropriate either before or later. This can apply to individual health issues as much as to human relationships and challenges. These realities, therefore, need to be borne in mind, both when receiving and acting upon any advice or guidance received from spirit guides.*

I then went on to outline a number of approaches for testing any teachings received from our or other's guides. In brief, these included doing searches of similar published works, seeing if the application of any practical advice or suggestions actually work, and of course, through the direct receipt of our own conscious communications with guides. Really, the main point is that one should be prepared to think critically for oneself and to ask relevant questions of any information thus received. In my experience, the guides do not object to this strategy and can even welcome the opportunity to make clearer and more transparent the teachings or advice they are transmitting to us. Certainly, in the five previous books that I have written with the help of my guides, healthy questioning of telepathically received contents has been a central feature.

I would go so far as to say that it would be unwise simply to accept everything brought through from *any* spirit sources without giving it due consideration and thought. Just as we need to exercise some discrimination and discretion when trying to make sound qualitative or value judgements about any given contents in daily life, the same should apply to spirit communications. Whether these communications are made by thoughts, words, images, sensations,

---

* Woodward (2018) pp. 13 – 14.

impressions, or clairvoyant faculties. If we can also confirm what-ever is received by reference to a number of independent sources, then our sense for the reliability and truth of such contents can be that much stronger.

What I am advocating here should not be misconstrued as having distrust or scepticism towards our guides, but rather as being reflec-tive of doing good research. After all, we know just how easy it is in ordinary life to get 'the wrong end of the stick', and to misinterpret what others say to us. Sometimes, the real meaning they are trying to bring across is completely lost, and this can lead to a lot of confusion about what was actually intended. So, to 'test the spirits' is, I think, healthy all round. Anything at all dogmatic or authoritarian is to be avoided. But let's now see what the guides themselves think about all this.

Bob: Joshua, can a guide comment on the theme of 'confirmations', please?
Joshua: Shalom, my friend, yes, let me comment on this for you please.
Bob: Thank you, please do.
Joshua: Yes, my friend, this is an important theme because it is indeed good to seek confirmations, or confirmatory evidence, you could say, of what is given from spirit sources. Why? Because there are beings, spirit beings, who do try to deceive and mislead those living on the earth plane. Of course, genuine spirit guides will not indulge in such practices, but you can never be too careful.

So yes, my friend, we agree with you that in doing research into spirit realms, one should always seek for corroborative evidence. In this way, the possible pitfalls can be avoided, and thereby, a much greater sense of certainty will be obtained. As you also rightly say, this does not mean in any way that trust in your guides is dimin-ished. However, the process of communication is a subtle one, and discrepancies can creep in quite inadvertently. So again, for this rea-son, it is always good to use every means of checking the accuracy of what has been received.

Having said all this, we would not wish to dissuade any genuine seekers after truth from making contact with their guides and friends in spirit. When this comes about in the right way, it is a truly cooper-ative endeavour on both sides of the veil, and can result in much help and support being given. So, with this I think I have made our view on this matter clear. Take precautions, proceed carefully, but know that you can put your trust in your guides to do the best they can to give you information that is reliable and trustworthy. All blessings, Joshua.

Bob: Thank you, Joshua, for that. This leads us to our next theme, in which we can become clearer about the nature of guides *per se*, and their roles.

Guides

Who or what are spirit guides? This is clearly a key question in the context of this book. Essentially, as I understand it, this term mainly refers to discarnate human beings who, from spirit worlds, are willing to be of help and support to those of us who are still earthbound. Now, having said this, I also realize that spirit guides can be understood in a much broader way. That is to say, to encompass spiritual beings, on a variety of levels, who can help guide us in various ways. So, for example, we can well describe our own angel as such a guiding being for each one of us. Or, we can refer to certain archangels as having the task of leading whole groups of people, in terms of different races and nations. Perhaps yet higher beings, also belonging to the so-called spiritual hierarchies, can extend their influence yet wider over humanity.

In my book *Knowledge of Spirit Worlds and Life after Death* (2020), Chapter 4 was entitled 'Spirit Guides'. The format of the chapters in this particular volume was in the form of questions and answers, rather than first receiving teachings *per se*. So, I was asking the questions and one or another of my guides gave the answers. As Chapter 4 was very informative and detailed, I would, of course, encourage readers to study it carefully. However, for our purposes here, let me just try to summarize some of the main points that came through. Whilst my own guides acknowledged that various beings of the spiritual hierarchies did act as guiding spirits for humanity, I kept the main focus in that chapter on those who especially supported us as individuals. For example, such spirit guides can be, and perhaps often are, departed family members. However, as my guide Raja Lampa pointed out, such family connections should be received in the broadest sense, since we have all had numerous earthly lives. Therefore, our extended family includes many people.

Another important point had to do with the specific roles which guides take on. For example, if a person is involved in healing or therapeutic work, then they would attract the attention of guides who have a certain expertise in this field e.g., Dr John and his team of spirit doctors. Or, guides can take on more of a teaching role, and help with an individual's efforts in developing themselves inwardly on a spiritual path. There again, as my guides indicated, if a person is engaged in some branch of science, then guides who could inspire and assist that particular calling would be attracted. And so on, say with an artist or craftsman, or whatever. In short, particular guides are around people to offer help in every way that is needed. However, such specialist guides might only draw close to that person in order to render help on some particular problem or issue. In other words, guides can come and go, depending on the circumstances and needs. Nonetheless, each person, as I understand it, will have a main guide, who remains close to them over a longer time, perhaps for a lifetime. For example, Ruth White describes in her fascinating book *Gildas Communicates* (White and Swainson, 1971) many years of cooperative work with Gildas as her main guide. I recall an evening arranged in Cheltenham by Iris Ratsey, where Ruth demonstrated her mediumship in bringing through teachings from Gildas. In her more recent book, *Working with Spirit Guides* (2004), Ruth writes:

> It is now over 46 years since my serious channelling of Gildas began, and the work has become a joint work. My life and training have given me skills in working with people and running workshops. Gildas provides the extra dimension of information. We are a team that works with great harmony and mutual respect. He is always near me, just as he was when I was a child.*

Another very well-known example of a main guide working with a medium is White Eagle, who transmitted teachings through Grace Cooke. She was already well aware of White Eagle as a child.

It's true that, in these two examples, the teaching role of the guide was very clearly shown. Nonetheless, for all of us there does seem to be a certain main guide who has our best interests at heart and stays with us for a relatively long time, although I didn't meet my main guide, Joshua, until I was 58 years old. Perhaps, after some years, we may receive a different main guide? I'm not sure about this, however, and would need to ask that question. So, let's do that now.

---

* White (2004), pp. xii-xiii.

Bob: Joshua, I understand that each person has what we call a main guide, i.e. a spirit guide who stays with that person more long-term than other guides who may come close for some reason and then move on. But I wonder, Joshua, whether main guides also change over sometimes? Can you tell me?

Joshua: Shalom, my friend. Yes, that is possible. Everything really depends upon the needs of the person whom they are helping or supporting. Very often, the main guide is there for a longer period, say for many years, but if there is a need for a change, then another guide can assume that role.

Bob: And what sort of need might necessitate or influence such a change of guide?

Joshua: Well, if the person in question is entering into a quite new phase of life and needs a different kind of support than their main guide has hitherto provided for them, then another guide could offer to take on that supporting role. Remember, my friend, that on our side of life we work in teams rather than individually, so this enables us to respond to different needs as and when they occur.

Bob: Right, I can see what you mean, Joshua. So, could this also happen with me in respect of you supporting me?

Joshua: Well, it could, but in your case, my friend, we think it unlikely, because we have a specific work to do together in writing your books. Of course, you do the actual writing, but I'm helping you with this work, as well as the other guides who have made themselves known to you.

Bob: Yes, Joshua, and as you know, I usually call upon you first if ever I have a question, or in order to gain some confirmation.

Joshua: Shalom, my friend. This is true, and I am happy to be of service to you in this way. All blessings, Joshua Isaiah.

*

So really, the most important thing to grasp when we speak of 'spirit guides' is to know that they do actually exist, and that their sole concern is to be of genuine help to each of us. Therefore, if we can learn to link up with them consciously, we can open the door to a very fruitful and cooperative way of working. In the early twentieth century, Rudolf Steiner indicated how those who have died can become the 'counsellors' of the living (those still in the body, that is). It seems to me that this is indeed a common task of spirit guides, but it falls on us to develop the receptivity and sensitivity towards the counsel and advice that they willingly give us. Let us just see if one of my guides would like to comment on this.

*

Bob: Joshua, would someone like to step forward for this?

Joshua: Shalom, my friend. Yes, Red Cloud would like to say something to this.

Bob: Right, Red Cloud, please do.

Red Cloud: Hau, my friend. Yes indeed, it is the task of guides to be of help in every way that they can. If only more people would be aware of this, then there would be greater opportunity to make ourselves heard. However, too often there are no ears to hear us. In spite of our efforts to come through in order to give counsel, advice or teachings, those on your side of life remain blind, deaf and dumb, so to speak. This can be quite frustrating for us in spirit worlds, when all that we wish to do is to help people deal with their daily lives in a better, more harmonious fashion. Therefore, we are more than happy to cooperate with you, Bob, when you do your writings, because we hope that this will help those who read your and our words to become awake to these realities. We do appreciate, of course, that people are very busy dealing with all that meets them in their daily lives on earth. Nonetheless, it is a fact that we, the guides, are there to help when called upon. However, we are very dependent on initiatives coming from your side of life. We must and do respect your own free will. With this I feel I have made the contribution which I wish to make, and I thank you for it. All blessings, Red Cloud.

Bob: No, thank *you*, Red Cloud. What you have brought is very important for this chapter. Thank you again.

I think that we are ready to move on to the last chapter in Part I of our book, and turn to the theme of 'Gratitude'.

Gratitude

I feel very grateful to Anne Lewis for the part she played in making me aware of my spirit guides. It is said that doors can open for us when the time is right. I think that is true, whether we refer metaphorically to 'doors', or speak of certain opportunities that present themselves to us. Certainly, the opportunity to meet Dr John and, a little later, Joshua Isaiah, has since then had a very significant impact on my own life and its direction.

Whilst I had believed in the reality of spiritual worlds of spirit beings long before contacting Anne, to be given the opportunity of actually developing conscious communications with discarnate souls brought my inner experiences to a new level. It is, after all, one thing to read descriptions of spiritual realities, for instance in the books and lectures of Rudolf Steiner, but it is another thing altogether to begin to enter into communion with those who live in spirit worlds. This form of communion, as I experience it, is what I have referred to as 'mental telepathy', the clear receipt of thoughts entering my mind, with the knowledge that these thoughts are not from me and my own thinking process. And that is where the introspective discrimination between one's own thinking and receiving the train of thoughts of another comes into play.

To have a feeling of deep gratitude for the opening up of such communications is very appropriate. This feeling carries the realization that one's guides are willing to be of support and help to us, even when we may feel rather unworthy of their friendship. By this I mean that on the spiritual path, which is really a path of self-knowledge, we are confronted not only by our positive potentials for growth and development, but also by numerous shortcomings and hang-ups! Especially if we are something of an idealist, the inner recognition of our faults and weaknesses can be hard to live with.

I can vouch for this through my own experiences, but can also imagine that what I have pointed to finds resonance in many others. There is no light without darkness, and the brighter the light, the stronger the shadow that is cast. I was struck by this fact not long ago, when out for a walk in the countryside on a sunny autumn day. Standing still with the sun behind me, I observed my own elongated shadow very clearly etched into the green grass. When a cloud passed over, my shadow vanished, only to emerge strongly again when the cloud disappeared. A simple observation to make, but one which in that moment spoke volumes. We all have such a shadow side to our inner nature, and the more one strives along the spiritual pathway, the more we can be confronted with this reality. There are times when, especially in a relationship with others, we need to be able to jump over our own shadow!

Precisely because of this dual inner nature of light and dark, we can feel very grateful when we come into conscious relationship with our friends across the threshold. They do not judge us, but wish to support us in every way that they can. Partly, of course, this depends upon our own willingness to accept their advice and counsel. As we have made plain before, there will never be any imposition or coercion towards us on the part of genuine guides. Therefore, it is a cooperation that is looked for, whereby both our guides and ourselves gain mutual benefit. If we include our own angel in this symbiosis, then our feelings of gratitude will be strengthened even more. To imagine or comprehend that this special spirit being has stayed by us through thick and thin, in order to help us to follow our own destiny, is a truly humbling thought. However, angels will be happiest if we can learn to cooperate with them on a conscious level, rather than unconsciously benefit from their ministrations.

We live in a time when these connections should become clear and transparent realities to us. So, to cultivate gratefulness and to extend our gratitude is to exercise a soul force or mood which helps bring about a concrete link with our invisible companions in life. Therefore, to take every opportunity we can to practise feeling grateful – grateful for small mercies, we could say – is an entirely positive thing to do. This might be, for example, by being thankful when we drink a glass of clean water, knowing that for so many people on the planet this would be a luxury. Yes, shocking though it is to express it like that, many things that we have access to in our ordinary lives would be seen as 'priceless' for those who do not have them. There is, therefore, no shortage of opportunities for us to be grateful, once we have made ourselves fully aware of all that we already possess.

This feeling can then provide 'the ground under our feet', so to speak, for our good interactions with friends in other worlds. At this point, we can invite one of my guides to step forward and comment.

Bob: Joshua, would a guide like to contribute to our theme?

Joshua: Shalom, my friend. Yes indeed, Markos would like to come in here.

Bob: Right, Markos, please do so.

Markos: Yes, my friend, what you are speaking of in this chapter is really important. It is essential to have gratitude for all that is possible once a conscious connection with us has been established. And this is a two-way feeling. We on our side of life are truly grateful when we are allowed to have liaison with those on the earth plane who seek our help and guidance. As you have said, my friend, this help will never be in the form of any imposition or in reducing the free will of our human co-workers. No, indeed, this recognition of each person's free will is absolutely essential. However, that being said, when you find ways whereby a true cooperation, a true working together, can come about, then this is a lovely thing to behold. If only this would happen more, then many problems and difficulties would be shared and hopefully resolved. Just the fact that people begin to realize that there is more to life than what they just see around them with their physical eyes and can touch with their physical hands, is already a huge step to make. But to go so far as to realize that there is a support network already in place, spiritually speaking, is a further step of reassurance and comfort. This realization is another strong source of gratitude for what is around everyone and is ready to help them through their lives. So, my friend, with this you yourself are helping to make others aware of the realities in which you all live, with us and with your loved ones in spirit worlds. All blessings, Markos.

Bob: Many thanks, Markos.

On this note, we bring this last chapter to a close, and with it the various themes which we have addressed in Part I.

47

Conclusion to Part I

In a small book entitled *The New Mediumship*, which was first published in 1965, Grace Cooke, the medium for White Eagle, gives a description of the ongoing development, or evolution, of mediumship. Based as it is on her own 60 years of experience, Cooke's book makes for an informative read, both about the possible pitfalls of various mediumistic practices and of the positive potentials for genuine and reliable methods of communication across the threshold. For example, she writes:

> Psychic phenomena have been changing during the last 25 years, and we have seen a gradual strengthening and development of the mental side of mediumship.*

Included in what she calls mental mediumship are trance control, clairvoyance, clairaudience and telepathy. She herself, when speaking as the mouthpiece and communicator for White Eagle, was clearly in some degree of trance. Now, as I have said previously, I do not enter into any trance condition when communicating with my spirit guides or with others who live in spirit worlds. I do not necessarily want to criticize trance mediums *per se*, since, as in the case of Grace Cooke, very helpful and, to my mind, genuine spiritual teachings can indeed come through. Nonetheless, as far as I'm concerned, fully conscious mental communications are the most appropriate method for our modern times. And this is what I have referred to in this book as the practice of mental telepathy, in the sense of receiving very clear thoughts from those in spirit worlds.

There seem to be other published examples of precisely this form of telepathic communication. In the book *Testimony of Light* by Helen Greaves, published in 1969, she describes how she was contacted by her deceased friend, Frances Banks. In the Foreword to this book, by Lieutenant-Colonel R. M. Lester, we read that:

> Telepathy between the living is now generally accepted, but telepathy between the living and the so-called 'dead' is

---

* Cooke (1985), p. 11

less common. Countless books have been written recording alleged communication with discarnate minds, and many of these are very dubious in their authenticity.

Such communications are claimed to have been received by a variety of methods – automatic writing; clairaudience; trance mediumship, and so on.

The highest level of communication is undoubtedly that of telepathy, and in this book, we have an outstanding example of this, where communion between two people on either side of the veil has been achieved without effort – and without seeking – in a very beautiful manner.*

Helen Greaves and Frances Banks were intimate friends and – for the last eight years of Miss Banks's life – the two of them worked together psychically and spiritually. Thus, they had built a strong spiritual connection in earthly life.

Another example of conscious telepathic connection with a deceased individual is given in the book *The Bridge Over the River*, published in 1974 in English translation. This referred to communications received over a period of just over five months, in the year 1915. The subtitle of the book is: 'Communications from the Life After Death of a Young artist who Died in World War One.' This artist, a promising musician by the name of Sigwart, was able to contact one of his sisters with whom he had an intimate connection. Regarding this sister we read:

> After some time, however, an inner awakening enabled her to establish contact with her brother in full consciousness. She described the experience thus to another sister: 'In the seclusion and quietness of these past days, I have come to recognize what Sigwart expects of me, which is not to guide my hand and influence it externally; rather, I myself must open a door in my mind; then I shall hear the words I have to write down.†

---

* Greaves (1969), p. 7.
† Wetzl (1974), p. vi.

In November 1915, Sigwart's sister decided to show Rudolf Steiner the communications she had received. After careful scrutiny, Steiner apparently said:

> 'Yes, these are exceptionally clear, absolutely authentic communications from the spiritual world. I see no reason for dissuading you from listening to them further.' He added that transmissions of *this* kind are very rare.*

Well, I wonder what Steiner (1861–1925) would have to say about the various communications from my spirit guides, which have been published since 2005? I can only add that I believe them also to be genuine telepathic transmissions. Perhaps such contacts are no longer now as rare as they were in Dr Steiner's day?

A recent example of such transmissions are the illuminating conversations between two sisters. The older sister, Ajra Pogacnik, died in 2011. In the book, *Being Human in the Now*, Ana, the younger sister, shares the various conversations with the soul-being of Ajra. She writes,

> I am able to sense Ajra's presence directly and to communicate with her inwardly. I do not hear her voice, I do not see words, but I can write down her message as thoughts that flow rapidly towards me. Whilst I am writing – when I am directly in the flow – it does feel to me as if it were my own knowledge. But I know that they are not my thoughts, because also for me some things are new and surprising.†

Her description seems very similar to my own way of receiving messages from my spirit guides. One of the main themes in their book is the need for those of us who are presently incarnated to feel connected, united, with those human souls living in spiritual dimensions. Thereby, to overcome the seeming separation caused by physical death, by knowing that life continues in the spirit. I think that working with our spirit guides helps us towards such a realization

The purpose of this section of my book, as I wrote in the Introduction, was to share something of my own experiences in learning to communicate with those who live in spirit worlds. This was done in the hope

---

* Ibid., p. vii.
† Pogacnik, A. (2022), p. 9.

that it may perhaps be of help and encouragement to others. I have described the themes which, in my experience, belong to this method of fully conscious communication. Namely, Intentionality, Silence, Thinking, Trusting, Identities, Conversations, Safeguards, Cooperation, Confirmations, Guides and Gratitude. I explained that these themes were derived from an analysis of what actually belongs together and forms a wholeness in this particular methodology. These themes were separated out in the various chapters simply for the sake of clarity and transparency.

Provided we have become very clear about our intentionality and motivations for wanting to establish conscious contact, the key skill is to learn to distinguish our own thinking, our thoughts, from the thoughts we receive from those in spirit. That is to say, to become able to accurately receive such telepathic communications. This conscious method may not appeal to everyone, and in such cases, provided your intentions are sound, then those in spirit may find other ways to make themselves known to you. It is only possible for me to attempt to describe here what has become a concrete reality in my own life. What *is* very clear is that our guides in spirit *do* wish to be of service to us and to help and support us in our earthly lives and inner spiritual strivings.

PART II

WORKING WITH YOUR GUARDIAN ANGEL

.

A Revelation

William Blake had been reading an edition of Edward Young's *Night Thoughts*, which he had agreed to illustrate, and had come to a passage in which the poet asks, 'Who can paint an angel?' Blake closed the book, according to his own account, and spoke aloud.

Blake: Aye! Who can paint an angel?
Voice: Michelangelo could.
He looked about the room but noticed nothing, 'save a greater
    light than usual'.
Blake: And how do you know?
Voice: I *know*, for I sat to him. I am the Archangel Gabriel.
Blake: Oho! You are, are you? I must have better assurance than
    that of a wandering voice; you may be an evil spirit – there are
    such in the land.
Voice: You shall have good assurance. Can an evil spirit do this?

Blake looked 'whence the voice came, and was then aware of a shining shape with bright wings, who diffused much light'. "As I looked, the shape dilated more and more: he waved his hands; the roof of my study opened; he ascended into heaven; he stood in the sun, and beckoning to me, he moved the universe. An angel of evil could not have *done* that – it was the Archangel Gabriel".'

Peter Ackroyd, Blake, p. 202.

Introduction to Part II

How did this new research enquiry come about? Well, on 14 November 2022, the day after Remembrance Sunday, I took down from my bookshelf a copy of *Angels at my Fingertips* by Lorna Byrne, in order to pass it on to my 11-year-old granddaughter. Some weeks ago, I had given her the first of Lorna's books, *Angels in My Hair*, and I know that she had enjoyed reading that volume. Therefore, I thought she would probably be keen to have this sequel too. I put the book down on a table in the sitting room so that I would not forget to pass it on to her.

After that, I went off to my local town to do some shopping. When I went back to the car after doing these tasks, I suddenly had the strong thought that I could write a book about my own communications with Philip, my guardian angel. Immediately on returning home, I took my pen and paper and wrote down the title and contents for this enquiry. I say 'enquiry' because I have always regarded my work with those in spirit as a form of spiritual researching, of posing questions and receiving answers. It took me less than ten minutes to choose the themes for the chapters and to write them on the Contents page.

I know that Philip is pleased with this project, because he has told me so. I also am enthusiastic about it because, I have to admit, I have tended to neglect Philip in comparison to my work with my spirit guides, especially with Dr John and Joshua. Having said this, in recent years I have had more contact with Philip than I did previously. Still, somehow I have found it easier to call upon my close spirit guides for advice, healing and teaching than to turn, consciously, to Philip. You might say that I have to an extent taken my angel for granted. That's not such a bad thing perhaps, because at least I knew he *was* there.

Lately, when I go to bed at night, I do ask Philip to guide me through spirit worlds when I leave my physical body behind on the bed, to remember who I've met and what I've done when journeying in spirit. So, I would say that I am certainly in process of working with my guardian angel, but I can imagine that this could go much further. Well, in this new next section in my book, we will together explore all this and see where it takes us. By 'us' I don't just mean Philip and myself, but you also as the reader of this book. If I can share my experiences of working with Philip, then this may help you to do something similar with *your* angel. I hope it can. Of course, that is assuming that you do actually want to get to know your angel and to find out how you can best cooperate with him or her, though I'm not sure whether it's really appropriate to speak of genders when referring to angels. That will be another thing to find out.

So, there we are. This is how this enquiry has come about – almost 'out of the blue' – because I certainly did not wake up with this idea today. However, as soon as the thought did enter my mind, I felt this absolutely was a good idea. I'm looking forward to seeing how this book will unfold – a bit like watching the unfolding of an angel's wings, if indeed they have them! Let us take this new enquiry as a journey of discovery and exploration – an important one since it concerns a spiritual being who has literally been at our side, perhaps watching our backs, for many thousands of years. As they say: 'A friend in need is a friend indeed'. It's time to meet and acknowledge our own very special friend.

As before, I'll first share some thoughts about the theme of each short chapter, before inviting Philip to share his views with us. Let us therefore proceed straight away and see these various themes as providing us with our 'doorways' for linking up with our angels.

Finding My Angel

I have previously related how I first became aware of my two main spirit guides, Dr John and Joshua Isaiah. This was through the 'Readings' that I received from a spiritual medium, in answer to my requests. These particular introductions were made in 2005. Later, I wrote my first book, specifically to do with my telepathic communication with John and Joshua. However, about a month before this book appeared, I met another medium through a mutual friend. She described herself as a 'trance medium', through whom her angel spoke. I met this lady towards the end of February 2007, and the first thing she, or rather her angel, said was, 'Do you know the name of your angel?' I replied that I didn't, and was then told that my angel's name was Philip. She added that he had wanted me to know this for a long time. When I needed to ask for help, I should speak to Philip.

This was my introduction to my guardian angel, which I had in no way expected when I went to visit the medium on that morning in February 2007. To be quite honest, the whole thing had taken me by surprise. Although, as a student of Rudolf Steiner's spiritual science or anthroposophy for many years, I had certainly long believed in the existence of angels, I don't think I had ever thought of them in terms of specific individuals with names – apart from, that is, the well-known traditional archangels, namely, Gabriel, Michael, Raphael and Uriel, connected with the four seasons of winter, autumn, spring and summer in the northern hemisphere. Well, later that day, I spoke with my guide, Joshua, about what the medium had said to me. I have kept a record of these communications in a notebook, and will share these with you now.

Bob: Dear Joshua, it was quite a meeting this morning with the medium, as I've never met anyone giving me advice so directly from spirit – from the horse's mouth, so to speak – there and then. Any comments?
Joshua: Shalom, my friend. Yes, you certainly put yourself right into it, didn't you! She has a direct line to spirit, and she brought through what spirit wanted you to hear. Yes, your angel, Philip, has been trying to get through to you for a long time, Bob, and he seized the

opportunity that the medium presented to you this morning. As he said, ask for what you want, or need rather, and it will be given to you one way or another. He is there to help you achieve your aims and goals in life. Do you want to speak to Philip now yourself, Bob? If you do, then just let him come through to you.

Therefore, for the first time, I did just that.

*

Philip: Bob, I am here with you. Never fear. I am indeed your angel, and have been your angel for ages past. It is I who walk alongside you and guide and help you on your chosen way through life. I am so pleased that you now know of me and can communicate with me as you do with your dear guide, Joshua.

Bob, avail yourself of me, remember me each day, until I can reveal myself as a sure presence to you. Feel me now next to you, behind you. I wish to work with you closely and consciously. I am so pleased, so glad, that now you know of me. Rejoice, my friend. Feel my presence. Feel my wings of light and warmth encircle you with love and strength, and let our relationship grow. Think of me each day, and I will do my best, my very best, my friend, to guard you and guide you on your way through life. Thank you for contacting me, and try to let yourself be open to my presence in your life. I am with you always as your higher guide and protector. Love and blessings in God's name. Yours, Philip.

*

Looking back now on this first communication that I had with Philip nearly 16 years ago, I can only feel grateful and reassured by his presence. But please remember, dear readers, I am in no way unique in having such a faithful companion. This is the lot of every one of us – you included! The only question is, 'How do we become aware and fully conscious of our spiritual brother or sister?' We will turn to that question in the next chapter.

At the time when I found this connection with Philip, my wife and I were going through some challenging and difficult experiences in our lives. This was due to our living conditions within a particular context.

Also, the meeting with the medium had raised some further questions concerning possible future developments. I therefore turned once again to Philip.

Bob: Philip, I feel somewhat at a loose end. Why? Because of the situation here that my wife and I have found ourselves in, but also because it is not clear to me yet how the healing work can or will develop. It is also not clear to me what I have to do with the medium, nor how I can develop the ability to see, sense, feel and hear spirit as others can. I seem only to have my telepathic link, but I do not see or feel! In short, I feel and wonder quite where I've come to and how it goes on. Any advice to give, please?

Philip: God's greeting to you, my friend and companion in spirit. You are confused. You know not which way to turn. You do not know how things will move forward for you. Do not fear. You are watched over. You are guided and being prepared to do great things, my friend and companion in spirit. Yes, 'companion', I say, because we have been together for many eons. Ages of time. It is your destiny and mine to be together in all ages of time to come. You wish for advice. The advice I give to you, my friend and companion, is to ask for the help you need. Ask and you will receive. Ask and it will be given.

*

Well, I have shared the above because I think it is good for all of us to know that we are actually being supported and helped, even when – or perhaps precisely when – we feel confused and rather lost. The key then, once we have taken the fact of our angel on board, is to be open to the help coming towards us. Though, I realize in saying this, that I have omitted the very thing which Philip emphasized. Namely, to remember *to ask*. It is asking which enables and allows the flow of help to stream towards us. Though Philip doesn't say it to me in the above communications, it must be because we have free will, as incarnate human beings, that the act of asking is so important. No spiritual beings, perhaps not even God, can help us without our free consent. I believe this is an essential issue which we must remember, especially when we feel most alone and isolated. 'Ask, and you will receive' is the promise given us in the New Testament. On this note, let us now draw this chapter to a close.

Finding Your Angel

Having described the event which led me to find my angel, Philip, in this chapter I'd like to explore how *you* also can find your guardian angel. Perhaps this will happen for you via contact with one or another medium, as was the case for me. But there may well be other routes to reaching the same goal. Obviously, in the first place we need to be open to the idea that we do in fact have an angel as our life companion. If we are closed to this notion and regard any talk of angels as simply superstition or fanciful and wishful thinking, then of course we will have no reason to explore this any further. Clearly, this doesn't apply to you, however, since you have read thus far.

So, in order hopefully to do justice to the theme of this chapter, I will enter into a conversation with Philip and ask for his advice and guidance. Who better to ask about angels than an angel? I have no idea, no preconceived notions, of what he may say, so this really is a research enquiry. Let us begin with our first question.

Bob: Dear Philip, are you willing to give us advice and guidance as to how to go about making a conscious connection to our angels?

Philip: My friend and brother, I am more than willing to give you the benefit of my advice on this matter. Have no doubt that the angels very much wish that their human charges be able to relate to them as close friends and companions.

Bob: Thank you, Philip. So, can you give us some ideas or suggestions as to how the reader of these pages can begin to make such a conscious link and contact with his or her angel?

Philip: Yes, my friend, there are various ways in which this can be done. As you have already mentioned, this contact may come about through another person, such as a medium or sensitive. That is to say, through someone who already has developed that awareness of the spiritual side of life, and is therefore able to be a go-between. That is certainly one possible way in which a conscious contact can be made. However, there are also many other ways in which this can come about.

Bob: Can you describe some of these other ways, please?

Philip: Yes, I can. Let us say, for example, that you meet someone. It may be someone that you know already, or it could also be a complete stranger. In talking to this person, you realize that something special happened to you, yesterday perhaps, or sometime before. In other words, you become aware, through your meeting or conversation, that something occurred that was really quite special. You also realize that if you hadn't met this person just at that moment, that this special event could have passed you by in terms of your awareness. But, through the meeting, you do realize the significance of that event in your life.

On reflection, my friend, you see that the meeting with the other person was something of an 'awakener' for you. Just through this meeting, you woke up to something you would otherwise have slept through. Now, in this meeting, in this coming together with that other person, we can also see the guidance of your angel as well. Of course, it could be that *both* parties experienced an awakening, in which case the angels of both were at work! So you see, my friend, that in such an occurrence, it is possible to become aware of a certain divine guidance. A guidance coming from the angels.

Bob: Philip, this is certainly very interesting, but even though a person, through the meeting with another, can become aware of the specialness of an event or occurrence, this doesn't mean that they will automatically think of the involvement of an angel, does it?

Philip: Quite true, my friend, but it begins to alert someone of how they can learn of something which would otherwise have passed them by. In that sense, it is an awakening experience.

Bob: Yes, but they might not link this in any way with divine, angelic intervention.

Philip: No, they might not, but it does begin to help the person in question to become that much more open to such things. That is already opening up a door towards awareness of their angel.

Bob: Well, Philip, thank you for this. I wouldn't have thought of such an example myself. You said that there were many ways in which a contact with someone's angel can come about. Can you describe some more of these, please?

Philip: Yes, my friend, we can certainly give further examples of such possibilities. Let's say, for instance, that you are walking along the street and suddenly you stop in your tracks. You have no idea why. But nonetheless you just stand still. Sometime later, you learn that there was an accident not far away from where you stood, and towards which you were walking just some time before. You think to yourself, 'If I had not stopped, I might have been caught up in that accident', and you think, 'How lucky I was to have stopped at that moment'. Now, on reflection, the person may have the feeling or impression that they were being watched over, and, in a sense, protected. And indeed, in this instance, that was exactly what was taking place. In this example, we see again the working of that person's angel.

Bob: Right, Philip. So, I think what you're pointing us to with these examples is that in ordinary daily life we have an opportunity, or perhaps many opportunities, to begin to notice that certain interventions or influences are happening to us. Is that it? Is that what you're pointing out?

Philip: Yes, it is, my friend, and such things happen far more frequently than people might think. The angels are doing their best to guide and help people to live their lives in such a way that they stay clear of dangers and harmful events that would throw them off track.

Bob: Yes, Philip, but isn't it true to say that sometimes people need to go through difficult, maybe even dangerous, situations in order to meet their karma?

Philip: Yes, this is also true, and when that is really the case, then the angel will not interfere with that at all. However, there are many other instances when danger can be justifiably averted and protection given. In those cases, the angels are kept very busy.

Bob: Philip, can you give us further examples of when a person can become aware of their guardian angel?

Philip: Yes, Bob, I can, and as I have said, there are really many ways in which this can happen. Therefore, I can only provide you with some examples. It would be impossible to cover every instance because these are as numerous as there are individuals. Remember, it is very much an individual and personal experience for each person. Everyone is different and everyone is unique.

Bob: Yes, Philip, I can see that. So, what else can you tell us?

Philip: Well, my friend, there will of course be some people already who have some sort of awareness of angels, and perhaps also of their own angel in particular. This can happen when they are followers of one or another religion or spiritual grouping, or when they have a particular interest in spiritual or occult literature. Such people are already very open to contact with angels, simply because they are really interested in spiritual subjects. However, even with such people, it may be a big step for them to actually get to know their angel. You do find, my friend, that even with people who are very interested in spiritual matters, they don't make this step to actually engage consciously with their own angel. Their interest remains on more of an intellectual or even abstract level, rather than penetrating right down into everyday life. And it is, my friend, in everyday life, in very practical situations, that the concrete contact with a person's angel is best met. Angels are not intellectuals, but practical helpers of humanity, so it is in practical, everyday life that such real contacts can be made.

Bob: Well, Philip, that's very interesting. However, I must stop for now, and would like to continue this theme with you later. Is that all right?

Philip: Yes Bob, that is perfectly all right with me. I will await your readiness to pick up our conversation. All blessings, Philip.

*

Bob: Right, Philip, I've sat down to work with you again. Let me ask this question: Would it be easily possible for people to communicate telepathically with their guardian angels as we are doing now?

Philip: Well, my friend, you need to realize that you do have a special ability in this sense. We know that you don't think of yourself in that way, but nonetheless you have developed the ability to distinguish your thoughts from ours in a way that others could find very difficult to achieve, at least with any certainty. So, in answer to your question, we would say that telepathic contact is possible, but often not easy to achieve.

Bob: Well, Philip, perhaps then it would be easier for someone to develop their clairvoyance in order to *see* angels. What do you think?

Philip: Here again, my friend, this is given mainly only to a few to practise. Yes, all things are possible, but in order to achieve something, work and effort are often required. It is true that some people do have a natural, inborn gift to see us. This can certainly be the case, but such people are few and far between. Such capacities will become more widespread in the future as humanity evolves, but at present such natural seers are the exception rather than the rule. Having said that, children are often much more open and accessible to seeing angels, though the grown-ups may scoff at such things.

Bob: So, what about receiving physical signs of their angelic presence? Some people seem to swear by white feathers appearing. Is there any truth in that?

Philip: To an extent, yes, but it should not be taken too far. It is possible for an angel to initiate some sort of physical sign. Not necessarily a white feather, but maybe a feeling of warmth, or a gentle breeze that a person feels. Something simple, nothing too elaborate or complicated.

However, rather than physical signs as such, it is much more common to have a feeling or intuition of being looked after, of being protected and cared for in some way. So, more on the intuitive level, provided the person concerned is open for that.

Bob: There are quite a lot of books about angels nowadays, books of people's experiences, which have been collected and put into one volume, for example. I can imagine that such literature also helps to open people's minds and hearts to such realities. Correct?

Philip: Yes, indeed, and we are very grateful when authors like yourself, my friend, write such books and share their experiences. These can then be the trigger for other people to also experience such things for themselves.

Bob: Well, Philip, I think that the chapters which follow on from this one will help readers to make their angelic connections, don't you think?

Philip: Yes, we do think that will be the case. The themes you have chosen will enable us to build on what has been said so far. This in turn will make it easier for people to feel the link, the connection, with their own particular angel.

Bob: Actually, Philip, just one more question before we move on. Is it helpful if someone can learn the name of their angel? As you know, this is what happened with me through my meeting the trance medium. So, is learning the angel's name a good place to start?

Philip: Yes, indeed. We realize that many people, even spiritually-minded people, may not have thought of this. Namely, asking for their angel's name. Nonetheless, if you can find or intuit that name, this gives then a point of focus for communications and contacts.

So yes, my friend, we would recommend that individuals seek out the name of their special angel friend.

Bob: And how can they best do that?

Philip: Simply ask, and see what name comes to you. Perhaps not straight away, but after some days and nights, a name may drop into your head and it feels right. When this happens, use that name as the focal point in order to start to work with your own angel.

Bob: Right, thank you, Philip.

Learning to Cooperate

In my previously published research, I worked in cooperation with my spirit guides. This working together, this mutual cooperation, was an essential feature of those enquiries. It is cooperation which spans both sides of that threshold that appears to separate the physical and spiritual worlds. Included in my use of the term 'spirit guides', which mainly referred to discarnate human souls, was also Philip as my angel. Therefore, when we now focus our attention upon the angelic realm and how we can build conscious connections with our individual guardian angels, the theme of cooperation remains entirely relevant.

Although our angels are there anyway, and we can take this as a given, the challenge is: How can we develop our awareness, our sensitivity, to take this reality into our consciousness? The main task, as I understand it, of our guardian angel is to help us to keep 'on track' – on track of those aims, intentions and goals that we each set for ourselves before embarking on our earthly incarnation this time around. If we take on board the concept of reincarnation, of re-embodiment of soul and spirit in a variety of earth lives, then our angel has had a great deal of practice in trying to do just this.

My understanding is that it is the *same* angel, the same guardian of our chosen destiny, who has been with us throughout the centuries and millennia. We don't get a new angel each time we reincarnate, but continue with our ever-faithful spiritual companion. When I speak with Philip shortly, I will also run these particular 'understandings' of mine past him and see if I am correct in my beliefs. I'm happy to stand corrected! But at any event, I do believe that I am right in thinking that Philip, like your own guardian angel, is doing his best to help me remember and act upon my aims and goals for this lifetime.

Our intentions have been formulated by us before our birth, whilst still living in the spiritual world after our previous earthly death. We have arrived at these personal goals through our insights and deeper knowledge of what is required to balance out our karma, i.e. our deeds from earlier lifetimes. This is essential for our process of spiritual growth, development and evolution as individual human beings of body, soul and spirit. Intrinsically, we are really spirit beings who, for a time, are clothed in earthly garb – our physical bodies of flesh and blood. The earth planet is the ground, or the school you could say, where we come to realize our karma and destinies, as well as playing our part in the ongoing transformation, or spiritualization, of the whole world.

It is, therefore, very important that we can fulfil our destinies as much as we can in each lifetime. Everything we do here makes a difference to the world for better or worse. However, most of us don't normally remember clearly what we actually have come to do! This agenda is covered over by a veil of forgetfulness, at least to a large extent. Perhaps some people do have a much clearer picture of what form and direction their lives should take, though they are probably the exception rather than the rule. But fortunately, there is someone who *does* have a very clear picture of what we've chosen as our mission and purpose in this life. That 'someone' is our guardian angel. He/she knows – has a memory – of the pathway we have decided to walk on planet earth. Therefore, the more we can learn to cooperate with our angel, the more likely we are to stay on task without being too often diverted along by-roads or ending up in cul-de-sacs. This is why we stand to gain a very great deal if we can establish conscious cooperation. I think this suffices for an introduction to this chapter, and it is now time to ask Philip to advise us further.

Bob: Philip, can you help us to understand how we can learn to cooperate and to work together with our angels?

Philip: Yes, my friend and brother, I can, and I am happy to give advice and suggestions how best to do this.

Bob: Thank you, Philip. In that case, I will take this conversation up with you in our next session tomorrow.

*

Bob: Right, Philip, I am ready with pen in hand to see how you can help us to understand how we can best cooperate with our angels. I'd like to just let you begin, Philip, and then see how we continue. Is that all right with you?

Philip: Bob, this is perfectly all right with me, and I will first give some advice on this theme. Now, in the first place, it is important to understand that the angels do wish to work together with their human charges. They wish for a conscious relationship to come about more and more, so that their work is more effective, more helpful to the human beings they are responsible for. When I use the term 'responsible', my friend, I am in no way suggesting that angels are dictating or controlling what happens with human beings. Far from it. We respect the free will which has been granted to you from God, and our aim and purpose is purely to be of service and help. We have no other ambitions than that, so there is no need for anyone to feel that their freedom is in any way compromised by working with us. However, we do value enormously the possibility for humans, in freedom, to turn towards us and elicit our help and support. In doing this, a clearer channel is made for such support to flow down to you than might otherwise be the case. If this sort of relationship and acknowledgement can come about, then there is a greater degree of true cooperation between us, between angels and human beings.

To enable this to happen, my friend, we need people to turn towards us in a mood of expectancy and gratitude. These feelings then enable us to respond in kind. We really take our cues from you, and in that sense we are dependent on human beings for what we are allowed to do. You see, my friend, how finely balanced is our relationship. We are servants to you as human beings. We do not wish to be in any sort of superior position, but only to be of equal value and proportion to yourselves. So, my friend, to summarize: the more that human beings will take the initiative, the free initiative, to work together with us, the better will be our cooperative relationship.

Bob: Thank you, Philip. I think you've made your points very clearly. So, as I understand it, the angels wait for us to initiate a truly cooperative working between us. Is that correct?

Philip: That is absolutely correct, my friend and brother. We await the approach of human beings, in order to enter into a closer cooperative working with them.

Bob: Well, this can't be easy then, considering how few human beings spend time or thought towards their angels? People are usually much more interested in earning their daily bread and enjoying themselves, I think.

Philip: Yes, my friend, what you say is true, and it is a certain sadness that the angels experience when, by and large, they are neglected by human beings. Nonetheless, of course they are true to their task and do everything they can to guide their charges along the routes they have already decided upon.

Bob: But if there really was a conscious cooperation initiated from our side of life, I imagine it would make our angels' work much easier and smoother to accomplish?

Philip: It would indeed, because often we face an uphill task in trying to keep humans on track with their pre-birth aims and goals. It can be, and often is, a very laborious task to help them follow their own destinies.

Bob: So, once again, could you just say clearly, Philip, what is required, what is needed, for us to be able to truly cooperate with the angelic realm?

Philip: My friend and brother, above all else, it is the recognition that you *do* have an angel watching over you. Just that fact alone, if recognized, would pave the way for a new form of cooperative activity and working to come about. It's rather like having a close friend on earth, isn't it? I mean to say, that if you have found a true friend, a good friend on earth, then you feel yourself supported and helped by this friendship. You help each other; it works both ways. It is not one-sided. Similarly, once you know that you have an angel as a true friend, you open up a relationship that is fruitful for both of you. It is mutually beneficial and nourishing. It is actually a relationship grounded in love. We need this relationship in order to perform tasks to the fullest possible effect, and you, in turn, will benefit from the help that we can give. So, we feel it is certainly something to aim for.

Bob: Yes, I agree with you, Philip, it is indeed a worthy goal to aim for: the cooperation between men and angels.

Philip: Yes, but do include all the ladies, my friend! We make no distinction between human beings by the means which can divide you in earthly life. We treat all people as representatives of humanity, plain and simple.

Bob: Philip, thank you for making that essential point. There are certainly too many things which can and do bring about divisions and acrimony between people in earthly life. I think, Philip, I will bring this chapter to a close, unless you have anything further you wish to add?

Philip: No, my friend, we think what has been said here has covered what is essential. All blessings, Philip.

Bob: In that case, I will turn to our next theme.

Developing Trust

The theme of this chapter is particularly poignant to me. Why? Because it has been a real challenge for me to develop sufficient trust in myself and in my spirit guides over the years that I have worked with them. In my book *Spirit Communications*, published in 2007, I had a chapter called, 'A Doubting Thomas', which alluded to the disciple Thomas, who was not prepared to believe that the Christ had really transcended death on the Cross until he had gained his own first-hand evidence of Christ's resurrection. He needed, there-fore, to trust the evidence of his own senses, rather than rely on the accounts of others, that Christ had indeed risen. In that chapter, I can-didly wrote about my early efforts to receive telepathic communica-tions from my guides, as I began to build up trust in my own abilities and also in my guides' objective reality.

As I commented towards the end of that chapter,

> However, there is no doubt that in working consciously with Spirit, 'trust' is a key word and a key faculty, which needs to be developed and strengthened. Trust and confidence allow things to take place which otherwise are obstructed and sti-fled by distrust and doubts.*

I also made the point that what is required is not some sort of 'blind' trust or faith, but rather an inner conviction born out of experience, humility and insight. In other words, it is an ongoing development of trusting, as one gets to know oneself and one's guides over time. This kind of trust also allows for critical thinking and questioning to take place. It has, in fact, been a key feature of my books, where I have brought through communications from my various guides, that invariably I question and challenge what they have said. Through this approach, I enter into a critical discourse with the guides, in order to gain as much clarity and transparency as I can about various themes. The guides not only have no problem with this strategy, but I would say they welcome it. I think

---

* Woodward (2007), p. 59.

there could be a possible danger in simply accepting, as a sort of gospel truth, what guides say, just because they live in spirit worlds. Genuine guides don't claim to be omniscient, and, in any case, there is always the possibility for unwanted errors to occur when receiving telepathic communications. Therefore, coming into lively discussions with them is one way of trying to safeguard the accuracy of what has been transmitted. Having said that, the development of mutual trust is really the sure ground which we can stand on, and in my case it was especially important to build this foundation.

Therefore, towards the end of *Spirit Communications*, when I wrote a chapter entitled 'Review and Looking Forward', I included the following:

> However, it is above all trust in oneself and in the spirit, and in the wise guidance that works into one's life, that has posed for me the biggest challenge and test. This comes through very clearly, emphatically I would say, in very many of the communications. Trust, trust, trust! This is not a matter of being asked to trust in a foolish or gullible way; it is rather to realize that trust in itself is a power – a power that opens doors.*

Well, I think it is now time to turn to Philip and ask for his advice on this theme. I will do this tomorrow.

*

Bob: Dear Philip, can you comment please on the theme of 'developing trust'?

Philip: My friend and brother, this is certainly a most important theme. Actually, trust is not an issue for the angels. Angels put their trust entirely in God and therefore it is already intact and inviolable. The matter of trust and its development is fundamentally a human problem or challenge, we could say. Nonetheless, or rather just because of this, it is indeed essential that a trusting relationship to one's angel can be built and established. Angels do not demand trust from their human charges, but they do long for

---

* Woodward (2007), p. 156.

this to be there. Through such trust, it is made very much easier for the angels to discharge their responsibilities and to guide human beings along their chosen pathways. So yes, my friend, to develop trust is indeed important.

Bob: Thank you, Philip. I think perhaps the greatest challenge is for a person to trust themselves, because in a way this needs to come first, don't you think?

Philip: Yes, my friend, it does. If a person can put no trust in themselves, then they are really in deep waters, so to speak. I mean by this that they are out of their depth and in danger of drowning. Why? Because trust provides the buoyancy, the lightness, the support which is needed to stay afloat when things are getting difficult. Trust enables a person to find the inner strength and inner certainty to keep going, to believe in themselves, even when others doubt them. Therefore, it is really the ground on which someone can stand.

Bob: So, Philip, is it a prerequisite almost for building up trusting relationships with others, including our own angels?

Philip: Yes, it is. Have faith and trust in yourself, and then you can have faith and trust in others.

Bob: Philip, what advice would you give for how we can develop a trusting relationship to our angel? What should we do?

Philip: My friend, first have trust in yourself, in your own motives and intentions. This is sacrosanct, we would say. If this is there, or at least being developed actively, then it should not be at all difficult to extend this trust to your angel too. Remember, my friend, that angels have implicit trust in their human charges. We do not judge, but we trust in the goodness, the inherent goodness, of people.

Bob: Well, Philip, that's really quite something to say! After all, some people may be absolute scoundrels and wish harm to others, and so on.

Philip: Yes, what you say is true. However, as angels we look to the core of a person, not to all the outer cloaks which they wear in life on earth. When we look to the eternal core, the spirit of the person, then we see that which has been given by God, and that is good. Therefore, we ever look to this goodness, and hope that the person can manifest this in their earthly life.

Bob: Well, Philip, that is something very profound that you have said. If only more people could know what lies at their own core.

Philip: Yes, my friend, it is our hope that this will become more and more available for human beings to acknowledge.

Bob: I think if they – if we – did, then it would help to change the world for the better, don't you?

Philip: We do indeed. To make the world good, you need to begin with yourselves, and this is precisely where we, as angels, wish to be of help and service to you.

Bob: So again, we come back to the need, the challenge, of making a trusting, trust-filled relationship with our angel. Correct?

Philip: Correct indeed. Once this has been built and established, then a great step forward has been made to realize the good that lies at the core of each person, each individual.

Bob: Well, Philip, it has taken me some time to develop trust in myself and towards my spirit guides.

Philip: Yes, it has, my friend. But you have shown that this can be done. You are doing this now by taking down the thoughts which I am sending to you. So, well done for this, my friend.

Bob: Thank you, Philip, for putting your trust in me. Actually, that's a very good way of putting it, isn't it?

Philip: It is, my friend, because, as angels, we are more than happy to put *our* trust into human beings, as this helps them to trust themselves.

Bob: On this very positive note, Philip, I will bring this chapter to a close.

Philip: Thank you, my friend and companion in spirit.

Strength in Life

There are some days when we may feel 'on top of the world'. Everything slots into place and things work out as planned – or at least, as we had hoped for. Under these circumstances, we can feel strong and self-assured. However, the opposite situation can and does also occur. We feel frustrated, limited, perhaps marginalized by friends and colleagues, and generally low in confidence and self-esteem. In other words, all of us have good and bad days. If we are lucky, then the good ones outweigh the bad. At any event, it is a fact of common experience that our feeling of 'strength in life' is a variable feast.

For example, if we have managed to achieve something after a prolonged effort, we can feel extremely pleased with ourselves, even elated. All manner of different areas of life could be the focus of our great success. This might be an academic achievement, some sporting prowess, a substantial financial gain, or simply very good personal relationships with others. Once again, though, the opposite scenario can unfortunately occur: disappointments at failure to achieve a certain goal; difficulties with others on a social or family or collegial level; an illness; feeling thoroughly depressed and worried, or perhaps an error of judgement leading to all manner of complications. Actually, it's just with all these latter scenarios that our need to find 'strength in life' is obviously more relevant than when everything is going well for us. But where do we find such inner strength?

For some people, this may perhaps come through their religious faith and beliefs. When the chips are down, they have their strong beliefs to fall back on to sustain them. For others, it may be the support of their good friends that sees them through the tough times. However, for those who do not have a strong supportive belief system, or lack real friends to call on when troubles come their way, the situation can be very grim. It may lead to desperation and despair, to self-rejection, and even, perhaps, to suicidal thoughts. Instead of experiencing strength in life, there is just a gaping void and a personal, dark abyss to face.

We do know that there seems to be an increase in issues connected to mental health nowadays. The recent Covid pandemic has certainly exacerbated incidences of illness, of a mental or emotional nature, compounded by difficulties in adequate referral services and overstretched medical provisions. Many people do feel desperately lonely and isolated. If only there was a much more widespread knowledge and awareness of our own guardian angels, as our ever-faithful friends and companions, who are always with us, come hell or high water! This is where books such as those by Lorna Byrne can be worth their weight in gold – precisely because in their pages we can learn about the real spiritual support which is always there for each of us! To just know of this, even though we may never actually see our angels (as Lorna clearly does), can begin to provide us with a real sense of 'strength in life'; a strength which comes from knowing that we are indeed cared for and, in fact, loved unconditionally.

Yes, angels may be sad when we go astray, and especially if we do harm to others or ourselves, but they will never give up on us. They are God's messengers and our appointed guides, for this and all our lives. This thought, if taken seriously, really can be the anchor that keeps us grounded while we courageously face whatever life serves up to us. Actually, the more this reality of the angel, *our* angel, takes root in us, the stronger our feeling grows that our lives really do matter. This gives us a sense of purpose and meaning, even in our darker times, including the 'dark night of the soul'. We are, in truth, never abandoned or left alone.

Well, we've reached the point again where I think we should ask Philip for his advice on the theme of this chapter.

Bob: Philip, can you give us your thoughts on how we can find strength for life, especially so in the troubled times in which we all live?
Philip: Yes, my friend and brother, I will certainly share my thoughts with you and the readers of this book.
Bob: Thank you, Philip. I will tune in with you tomorrow, in the next session.
Philip: Yes, my friend, please do. I will look forward to this. All blessings, Philip.

*

Bob: Well, Philip, a new day has dawned. Can you tell us how we may achieve strength in life with our angels?

Philip: My friend and brother, this is a most important theme, for many people are struggling to cope with their lives nowadays. Let me say the following: Your angels are always ready to provide support and assistance. They are not, however, miracle workers. They also need to feel the acknowledgement and awareness coming from their human charges. Why? Because what is required is a truly cooperative working together. When this can come about, your angels can be most effective. Through your awareness of their presence, they gain further insights into how best to help you through your difficulties. Remember, my friend, that angels do not live in physical bodies. They have bodies of light. So, in order for them to understand, to comprehend and respond to the sorts of difficulties that you face in your earth lives, the angels also need your help. They need to know exactly where the problem lies, so that they can offer maximum support. In other words – and in the first place – a person needs to have some knowledge, some awareness, that they really do have their angel with them. This awareness provides the portal, the doorway, through which the angel can reach down and help the person in need.

Bob: Yes, Philip, I can see that such awareness and recognition really facilitates support and contact, but don't the angels help anyway, even if the person never gives a thought in that direction?

Philip: Yes, of course the angels are doing their best to help, but it does make an enormous difference if the human beings have at least some inkling that their angel is with them.

Bob: So, you're saying that in order to feel the 'strength in life' which our angels can give to us, we need to acknowledge them. Correct?

Philip: Yes, that is correct. Then it becomes a real working together to solve the problems which are currently oppressing that person. The angel is in a much stronger position to help when *asked* to do so. But the asking only happens when a person realizes there is someone there to ask! So, this is what we mean by having some angelic awareness.

Bob: Philip, what you say does make sense in the same way that it's only if we ask a friend to help us out that they become more aware of the problem.

Philip: Precisely, my friend, a difficulty that is shared becomes much easier to tackle and eventually overcome. Therefore, your angel needs to know *how* best to help you.

Bob: And what sort of help can be given, since angels don't have their feet on the ground? They're not enmeshed in earthly life.

Philip: Yes, it will largely be soul help, we can say. That is to say, to be able to bring encouragement and upliftment to those who are struggling. But also, they can help to bring about meetings with others on the ground who can offer help. In this way, they can really steer a person towards those who are in a position to offer help.

Bob: So, to summarize, Philip, when we need to feel 'strength in life', strength to deal with all that weighs us down, the angels can be our inner support – our friends when in need, so to speak.

Philip: Yes, Bob, quite literally, we are friends who have stood the test of time.

Bob: I can also imagine that our angel may be able to give us the inspiration that we need. I mean, to get the best ideas to find solutions to our problems?

Philip: Indeed, they can, and this is one of the most important ways they can help, to inspire into you the idea that gives you a clue as to how to solve your problem. Yes, this is something most important, especially when your mind is chaotic or void of ideas.

Bob: Philip, I think we have probably covered this theme, don't you think?

Philip: Yes, Bob, I think we have. Strength in life comes from knowing that you are not alone, that your angel is always there constantly, to give you support and help.

Bob: Right, Philip, thank you. We will go on to our next theme in the following chapter.

Healing

The fundamental question when we turn to this theme is, 'Can angels help us to heal?' We will see what Philip answers to this question later.

Healing is of course a very wide theme to cover, since it belongs to at least several levels. Namely, the physical, emotional, mental and spiritual levels of being. As we have already mentioned, the mental aspects of healing and illness have taken on a much more public position than formerly, when a great deal of stigma was still attached to mental health issues. It was something of a taboo to admit to anything more than a bona fide physical, organic diagnosis. Fortunately, times have changed and attitudes have become more inclusive of problems occurring on different levels within us.

Another thing that has changed is seeing the doctor as the expert who has all the answers when something goes wrong with our health. The popularity of complementary, or sometimes alternative, approaches to orthodox mainstream medicine, showed that people want greater choices and involvement in their own healthcare. Together with this arose the many self-help books and programmes, whereby a person could be encouraged to participate actively in efforts to regain their health and strength. This was a much more participatory focus than just relying on 'the doctor' to make us better.

If we also take into account views of health and illness linked to such wide-ranging concepts as karma and reincarnation, we can perhaps begin to see that illness is not just a misfortune, but can also have deeper meanings for the individual. Through suffering a certain illness, a person may grow and develop in ways that they never imagined possible before. In that sense, to fall ill can be seen as an important part of that particular person's destiny in this lifetime. So, we see that there are various ways of viewing and indeed of going through our illnesses, and also of trying to treat them or even prevent them. The question in the context of working with our own guardian angel is to what extent, if at all, our angel can help us with our healing. And if so, on what levels of our being can this help be given? Is it somehow on the spiritual level, rather than necessarily having any impact on the physical, organic level of our human constitution?

As I once did a training as a so-called 'spiritual healer', more than 20 years ago now, I am very familiar with the paradigms of 'energies' interacting with our organic physiology and bodily functioning. There are different energies associated with our various chakras, for example, as well as life energy, or chi, flowing through our meridians. Energies can get blocked or restricted, instead of flowing normally.

A good friend of mine, who was clairvoyant and a therapist, made a very detailed study of the structure and functioning of the human energy field or aura. He was of the view that even so-called physical illnesses originated in the higher auric layers. These disturbances then permeated down, over time, to affect the physical body and to produce the symptoms of illness. Therefore, if the origins in the auric field could be addressed early enough, then the physical symptoms might be averted. Spiritual healing is one way of trying to balance the person's energy systems and to restore health.

According to my clairvoyant friend, many illnesses start on the emotional, or astral layer of the auric field. In modern times we are used to speaking of fear, stress, worry and anxiety as emotional states which are detrimental to our well-being, especially so if they become chronic long-term conditions.

So, let us see if Philip can enlighten us about healing from the angel's point of view.

Bob: Well, Philip, can you?
Philip: I will certainly try to do so by bringing forward ideas and suggestions which you may find helpful.
Bob: Good, Philip, then I will tune in with you tomorrow about all this.
Philip: Very well, my friend and brother, I will look forward to our session. All blessings, Philip.

*

Bob: Well, Philip, can you give us your views regarding the angels and healing, and perhaps more specifically, about the role of our own guardian angels?

Philip: Bob, my friend and brother, let me say to begin with that angels can be instrumental in helping to bring about healing. However, this should not be looked at in too narrow a way. I mean, for example, that healing is sometimes needed when people are in dispute with one another. It is not that they are ill as such, not in any physical, diagnosable way, but rather that there is ill-will between them, leading to argument and discord. In such circumstances, their angels can try to bridge over their differences and help to bring about a peaceful resolution. So, this is one way of bringing healing to bear.

Now, if we look at physical illnesses *per se*, then the angels can to some extent also be helpful. It depends just how far the illness has progressed. As you indicated earlier, my friend, many illnesses have their roots in different levels of the energy field, the aura. When, for example, there are emotional causes for an illness, then it may be that their angel can help to resolve these causes before they gather momentum and descend deeper into the person's constitution. So, it depends very much where the disharmony is situated as to how much their guardian angel can help. On the other hand, my friend and brother, there are also so-called 'angels of healing', who take on a more specific role in helping those who are ill and suffering. They can use energies, colours, fragrances even, to help overcome a particular illness. They have been given their task, their role, by higher powers and they can use them to help when other angels may be unable to.

Bob: So, actual 'angels of healing'?

Philip: Yes, they are a special class of angel, we can say, who have received special dispensation for their powers from higher ranks of beings.

Bob: Do you mean from archangels, or perhaps still higher beings?

Philip: Yes, my friend, I do. Both the archangels, the archai and yet higher ranks, or orders of beings, can send their forces through the healing angels.

Bob: Coming back again to our own guardian angels, unique for each human being, can they also help with healing?

Philip: Yes, we can, but as I have said, it does depend on what sort of level the initial trouble lies. Also, whether the illness is part of that person's special destiny situation. In that case, the healing may be more inclined to support the person through their illness, rather than trying to take it away. When it is a karmic illness, the guardian angel can help the person to bear it, and in doing so, to learn from the illness the lessons which it teaches.

Bob: This is, of course, very important, Philip, since, as you say, the illness in that case is there for a good reason. Correct?

Philip: Yes, indeed, my friend. The illness has a particular mission, you could say, to help the person progress along their evolutionary path and to achieve something which they otherwise would not.

Bob: And our guardian angels are really the 'protectors' of our destinies? Is this a good way to put it?

Philip: Yes, it is, but as well as offering protection, we also endeavour to help people to create new karma for the future. In other words, we are involved in a progressive movement forward, rather than looking backwards.

Bob: So, let's say, Philip, that someone is ill, whether that be a serious, maybe life-threatening illness, or a chronic-debilitating illness, or even a more minor affair. Is it a good idea to actually ask for help from the guardian angel?

Philip: It is always a good idea to ask for help, whatever the condition. Whenever a genuine call for help is made, there will be a response. So yes, in answer to your question: 'Ask and you will receive'.

Bob: Philip, a very specific question, please. Namely, can angels help us to heal when getting Covid-19, and also if we have adverse reactions to the vaccinations?

Philip: Bob, my friend and brother, these are more complicated scenarios to deal with, because other elements also have an impact on human beings under these conditions.

Bob: What do you mean by that?

Philip: Well, my friend and brother, other beings can insinuate themselves into human beings, and these can be very resistant to our efforts as angels.

Bob: Right. Nonetheless, if we ask for angelic help, it will be given?

Philip: Yes, without a shadow of doubt. Your angels will do everything in their power to help overcome the situation.

Bob: Can the archangels also help us?

Philip: Yes, they can, and it is good to call on them specifically.

Bob: Well, Philip, what you have said comes back again to people having some awareness of angels in the first place, doesn't it? If they don't, then it will not occur to them to ask at all.

Philip: Very true, my friend, and therefore the importance of this book and of other books which seek to enlighten people of our existence in their lives. Well done for that, my friend. Let us hope that what we are doing here will be of service to others, God willing.

Bob: Yes indeed, Philip, I also hope so. On this note, I'll bring this chapter to a close and then be ready to turn to our next theme.

Philip: Thank you, my friend and brother.

Bob: Actually, Philip, can I just ask you a couple of questions that might well be plaguing some readers?

Philip: Certainly, my friend and brother, please do.

Bob: Well, Philip, some people will be puzzled that I call you 'Philip', and the notion that angels have names. What do you say to them?

Philip: The names we assume are of course for your benefit. It enables you to focus your attention on us. So yes, you might say that these are names of convenience, but they do have a very clear purpose in mind. After all, you also, Bob, have had many names over your incarnations on earth. So, our names, like yours, fulfil a purpose.

Bob: Thank you, Philip. The next question is the gender of angels. Aren't you beyond any genders?

Philip: Yes, in a sense we are, but as your friend Michael just suggested to you, our energies can have a more masculine or a more female character. In that sense, it is justified that you think of us in these terms.

Bob: Right, Philip, thank you for clarifying these two points.

Awakening Consciousness

W hen we emerge from sleep each morning, we enter once again into our physical environment, and are aware of doing so. We may move from a deep 'empty' sleep, or from a state of active dreaming, into the light of self-aware consciousness of our body and our immediate surroundings. In other words, our consciousness awakens to the familiar world that we know and at the same time to a recognition of ourselves. All this is the stuff of daily common experience, and in this sense, it is not rocket science!

However, consciousness *per se*, exactly how it arises in us, and how its usual mechanisms may work, continues to be, scientifically, a 'hard nut to crack'.

> What is consciousness? Consciousness is the ghost in the machine. It is, for each of us, all there is: the world, the self, all experience. But the very subjectivity of consciousness makes it difficult to define, and harder still to characterise. How do our brains create conscious experiences and a feeling of being? Why do we have these sensations at all? These are unanswered questions that lie at the heart of the mystery of consciousness.*

In a footnote on page 74 of a 2022 *National Geographic* magazine (in an article entitled, 'The Brain – Discover the Ways Your Mind Works') we also find:

> For centuries, understanding human consciousness was relegated to religion and philosophy, and not a line of enquiry the natural sciences would tackle. Now, however, with increasingly sophisticated technology at our fingertips, it is considered the final frontier of neuroscience.

The only reason that I have included these references and given these short quotations is to point to the ongoing challenges which understanding our consciousness poses to modern science. Therefore, I also will

---

* *New Scientist Essential Guide, No.12 – Consciousness* (2022), p. 4.

make no attempt to try to elucidate these problems further in this chapter. I am certainly not qualified to do so.

Nonetheless, just as our awareness of the world around us does depend on being conscious, rather than unconscious in sleep, so our awareness of our guardian angels will depend on a certain 'awakening' of consciousness. That is to say, on some sort of enhancement of our so-called normal day-consciousness. If we acquire an ability to communicate with our angel, to perceive our angel, or to sense or feel our angel, this will surely mark a new step in our personal experience of our world. It will be an enrichment of what we have known before.

Now, as I have already explained, in my case communication with Philip is on the level of clear thought, through telepathic receiving of his thoughts in contrast to mine. Naturally, someone may argue that on this matter I am simply a prey to self-deception; that the thoughts which I believe are emanating from Philip are really my own constructs, my own concepts. To this I would reply that over the course of the past 17 or so years, through my repeated contact with my various spirit guides, as well as with Philip, I've become convinced of this process of telepathic communication with genuine spirit entities. For me to first become aware of this signified a certain inner awakening of consciousness, beyond what I knew before. And that is why I have included this particular chapter in this enquiry. It indicates that our human consciousness is well capable of expanding, of growing, to bring into our awareness other realities – in this particular instance, our angels. Let us see, therefore, if Philip can now throw further light for us on this essential theme. It is clearly essential because, without our consciousness, we simply cannot be aware of anything, either in the material sense world or in the non-material spiritual worlds.

Perhaps, through entering into higher states of consciousness, we can even explore the farthest reaches of the universe without the need to go into space physically by means of rockets? Then we may find that the universe teems with life and is inhabited by many sorts of beings, the angels included.

Bob: Philip, can you give us the benefit of your advice on the awakening of our consciousness in relation to our knowledge of the angels?
Philip: Yes, my friend and brother, I can. It is, as you say, essential for consciousness to be raised, to be heightened, in order for you to have

an awareness of your angels. This can come about in the first place by being open and receptive to angelic presences, to having an open mind in that respect. This attitude then enables the angel to also draw close to you. Whether a person then senses, feels, or even sees his or her angel will depend entirely on the possibilities of that person. It can be different for each person.

However, once a rapport has been established, once contact has been made, then this will enable a greater awareness to come about. So you see, my friend and brother, that the angels will take every opportunity offered to them to get their messages across.

Bob: Can you say more about how a person's conscious awareness can be heightened?

Philip: Well, this can be achieved by various means. Meditation and inner practice, to be receptive to subtle changes in the surroundings, are ways to nurture such a heightening of awareness. If a person is genuinely seeking to make contact with their angel, then you can be sure that the angel will respond likewise.

Bob: This awakening can take different forms?

Philip: Yes, it can, and as we have said, this depends upon the possibilities inherent in each person.

Bob: Is it correct to call it an awakening of consciousness?

Philip: Yes, it is, Bob, because it enables that person to become awake to a reality that up to then has passed them by. Just as a shock or surprise, say, can also cause a person to wake up, so this comes about when an angelic contact is made.

Bob: In my case, it is very much through receiving thoughts. Would this be similar for someone else?

Philip: It could be, but not necessarily. It could also just be a feeling, a strong feeling perhaps, of being watched over; being cared for and protected somehow.

Bob: Why then is it primarily in the realm of thought for me?

Philip: Because, my friend and brother, this is the way that is most natural for you, for your abilities as a thinker. For someone else, it might be a more visual mode of contact that leads to their awakening.

Bob: At any event, whatever the particular mode of contact, it is an awakening – or could you say, perhaps, a wake-up call?

Philip: It is indeed, and when it happens, the person involved feels very grateful for that experience.

Bob: And the angel?

Philip: The angel certainly, because every guardian angel wishes for a closer and more conscious relationship with his or her human charge.

Bob: How is that then with a so-called trance medium?

Philip: Well, in that special case, the person's consciousness is lowered from the everyday self-aware consciousness to a more dreamy state, we would say.

Bob: In that case, would we still speak of an awakening?

Philip: Yes, we could, but it is on a qualitatively different level compared to someone who has *raised* their awareness. By raising their awareness or energy level, we could say they come into more direct contact with their angel. Remember, my friend, that angels are on a higher frequency, or vibratory level, than human beings normally are. Living in the dense physical body lowers the energy levels compared to the light bodies of angels.

Bob: This is interesting, Philip. So, perhaps we could say that an awakening of consciousness is accomplished by a raising of energies in that person?

Philip: Yes, that is correct. The energies are raised and so is the awareness.

Bob: Well, Philip, I think at this point we can draw this chapter to a close.

Philip: Very well, my friend and brother.

Creating Our Future

It is often said that the future lies in our own hands. If this is true, then that means that it is ours to create. Therefore, it is neither fully predestined nor already known, but really it is our own work of creation. This will surely then be inspired by our aims and goals in life and, certainly to some extent, also conditioned by the circumstances, restrictions and opportunities that our life presents us with. There is actually nothing more fascinating than to see how children grow and develop. Every educator is in a privileged position to be the guide, helper and, hopefully, a good example for the young.

It is really a huge responsibility that we carry, both as parents and teachers, to lead our children along life's path. Or, perhaps better said, to accompany them along their own unique paths. Whilst siblings probably do find themselves in very similar circumstances in the family they grow up in, we know just how different their personalities are likely to be. Each child is truly unique, and within each one lies dormant the potentialities that can, under the right conditions, gradually reveal themselves. Like the small seed planted in fertile ground that is warmed by the power of the sun and germinates, so what is first hidden in each human being can in time blossom forth. Education, rightly understood, is never a matter of just filling the young child with facts and figures, but rather in providing the optimum conditions for their own inherent potentials to unfold.

Now, from such a description, some may think that all the future possibilities for that person are therefore already there, embedded within their soul. In other words, that the future is already, provisionally at least, present in the child. There may well be some truth in this. However, whatever potentials or gifts are hidden in the individual, they will need to be nurtured, developed further and given expression in the course of that lifetime. Moreover, some people only discover certain inner aptitudes or talents much later in life. For example, I only became an author with the publication of my first (co-authored) book in 2000, when I was 53 years old, and it wasn't until 2011 that I was awarded my PhD at nearly 64!

And so it is for very many, if not all of us, that we are continually creating our own futures for as long as we live. This process must be, I think, of enormous interest to our guardian angels. They are very aware of our pre-birth resolutions, and of the aims and goals which we have set for ourselves for this new incarnation. Guardian angels have, I believe, the specific task of helping us to be true to our chosen destinies. But just how far we can actually realize our intentions and create our futures accordingly, always remains to be seen. All that our guardian angels can do is to faithfully serve the human beings that are given into their care. They must always respect human freedom, and therefore cannot coerce or force us to do anything against our will, including when we act against our own best intentions. Their only purpose is to support, guide, protect and help us, within the parameters that they have to adhere to.

Clearly, the more that we can learn to cooperate with our angel, the more effective and fruitful will be the support we can receive. So, we are truly the architects and creators of our futures, both individually and collectively. Nonetheless, by enlisting the help of our angelic companions, we do stand a much better chance of fulfilling our intentions and potentials, of creating our very best futures.

Let us then ask Philip for his views on this theme.

Bob: Dear Philip, in this chapter I am proposing that, as human beings, we are the creators of our futures. That what we become and achieve in any lifetime on earth depends on each of us. Do you agree with me, or do you hold a different view?

Philip: Bob, my friend and brother, I do wholeheartedly agree with you on this. Yes, as human beings, you do create your own futures. While it is also true that each of you has an angel at your shoulder, so to speak, this angel can only accompany you along your life's path. The angel cannot interfere with your decisions or choices, but only support and guide you from a higher viewpoint.

Bob: Nonetheless, would you also agree with me that if we can learn to listen, to follow the advice and guidance from our angels, we have a much better chance of fulfilling our own aims and goals?

Philip: Yes, on this point too I am in agreement with you. Your angels are there precisely to help you to stay on track – on course – with the aims and goals which each of you has set for yourself. This is the *raison d'être* for the presence of your guardian angel. It is God's will that this guidance and support is given to each one of you, and this is why it is so important to recognize and acknowledge your angel. By doing this, the angel is given more power to guide you aright, through this stronger relationship.

Bob: Yes, Philip, but don't our angels have this power anyway? Why should it make any difference whether we recognize them or not?

Philip: Well, my friend and brother, just imagine how that is in real life. If you have a potential friend, let's say, but you fail to recognize this person, then you miss an opportunity to receive the support which they can give you, that they want to give you. Your failure to see the friend means that you cannot take advantage of what they can offer you. And that is a pity. It is similar in the case of your own guardian angel. The more you recognize the presence, the existence, of your guardian angel, the easier you make it for the angel to influence you positively.

Bob: Yes, Philip, that does make sense to me. And can our angel help us to create our future?

Philip: Yes, your angel can do this with your permission. With your consent, the angel is given power to guide you along your own chosen route or pathway.

Bob: So, in that sense, it really does become a cooperative working together?

Philip: Yes, Bob, it does indeed, and this is for the benefit of you both.

Bob: So, while the future does lie in our own hands, angels can facilitate, can help smooth, our forward progress?

Philip: Yes, Bob, that is a very good way of putting it. We can help to smooth the path that you have decided to travel along.

Bob: Thank you, Philip. Is there anything else which you wish to add on this theme?

Philip: No, my friend, we believe that you have covered all that is important. It is the consciousness of working with your angel that is really the key point here.

Bob: Right, thank you again. On this note, I will close this chapter.

Gratitude

I think that cultivating feelings of gratitude is very conducive to entering into a conscious working relationship with our guardian angels. To contemplate that this particular spiritual being has been our faithful and constant companion through many lifetimes is a remarkable and impressive thought. To my understanding, we don't get a new angel each time we reincarnate, but it is the same one who remains with us. I will ask Philip later if I'm correct in this belief.

In everyday life, we each have many opportunities to practise feelings of gratitude. Whereas it is all too easy to bemoan our poor fortunes and our lack of this or that, to remember to be grateful for small (or large) mercies gives our lives much more qualitative value. We really do have ample opportunities to show our sincere gratitude and thanks. By doing so, our souls can take on a certain lightness and warmth, and this inner experience also resonates with a knowledge of our angel's closeness to us.

Sometimes, when we are going through a rather challenging time and things threaten to wear us down, we may also think to ourselves that it could actually be ten times worse! Such a thought gives us renewed strength to face up to and tackle the problems in front of us. Our angel will do all that is possible to lighten our load and to smooth the path. Indeed, perhaps it was our angel who gave us that strengthening thought? The more we can consciously cooperate with our angel's efforts on our behalf, the better things will be. Who knows just how many disasters have been averted over the years, or even daily, through the faithful service of our spiritual protectors? More than we might imagine, most likely. Let us now turn once again to Philip, to get the benefit of his good advice.

Bob: Is gratitude an important attitude, Philip?

Philip: It is indeed, my friend, because it also helps to make you more open to all the positive influences that come towards you. It is an attitude that is natural to angels, since we constantly feel gratitude to God for all that we are. Therefore, when human beings also cultivate this attribute, it does indeed resonate with us too. We are attracted towards such an attitude of soul, rather as the moth is towards the light.

Bob: Well, Philip, this is perhaps an unusual analogy, but it does make the point rather well, I think. I suppose, by contrast, that if a person is pretty ungrateful with their lot, that this does not exactly help their openness towards working with their angel?

Philip: That is true, my friend. This negative attitude closes them off from us and makes it very much harder to make our presence felt. Indeed, any negative attitudes act like a barrier towards having a close relationship with the angels. They experience such states as antagonistic to what they wish to achieve with human beings.

Bob: And what is that?

Philip: To serve them, my friend. To be of service and help to them. But an atmosphere or aura of negativity prevents the influences of the angels from being felt or easily received by their human charges.

Bob: So, if we really do wish to work consciously with our angels, we should make our attitudes and soul states as welcoming as we can?

Philip: This, of course, would be the ideal. However, the ideal is often not possible, and clearly when a human being is suffering and struggling with their life, we will do all we can to help, even when we have to fight against a dark cloud of negativity.

Bob: In other words, an angel remains true to its task, no matter what the conditions?

Philip: We do, yes, and we will perform our duty, our God-given duty, to the utmost of our strengths and abilities.

Bob: On that note, Philip, I will draw this to an end. Thank you.

Philip: Thank you, my friend and brother.

Miscellany

In this chapter, I want to ask Philip a variety of questions that I think any of us might wonder about. In fact, some of them may seem very naive indeed. So, without further ado, I will start.

Bob: Philip, are you willing to answer my questions now?

Philip: My friend and brother, I am more than willing to answer your questions to the best of my ability, God willing.

Bob: Good, thank you, Philip. So, do we have the same guardian angel with us through all our earthly incarnations, or do we perhaps get a new angel each lifetime?

Philip: No, my friend, you do not receive a new angel each time you reincarnate. Your guardian angel is chosen and appointed for you by God, and will be ever faithful to you through all your lifetimes.

Bob: Philip, it is often said that our guardian angel is at our back, is positioned behind us. Is this true?

Philip: My friend and brother, yes, it is true, but it could also be that your angel is at your side, or even standing before you sometimes. So, do not take things too literally.

Bob: Philip, do we ever share our guardian angel with anyone else? Or, to put it another way, is our angel solely for ourselves?

Philip: The guardian angel is specifically allocated to his or her human being and to no other. So yes, your angel is committed to you alone.

Bob: Philip, what do angels look like? I mean, if we as human beings could see angels, how would they appear to us?

Philip: This depends, my friend, on your abilities and your receptivity for supersensible impressions. Angels can appear to people in a variety of ways. For one, it will be as an experience of light; for another, it will be in a human form.

Bob: So, are you saying, Philip, that sometimes it may be possible to see an angel as we can a human being?

Philip: Yes, I am saying that, my friend. An angel can appear in human form to some people.

Bob: So, literally? I mean head, body, arms and legs, hands and feet?

Philip: Yes, all of that.

Bob: But what about wings then?

Philip: Not wings as you imagine them, my friend. No, rather emanations of energy, which could appear as wings if this is how they are looked upon.

Bob: So, are you saying, Philip, that how angels appear to us will partly depend on how we expect to see them?

Philip: Precisely, my friend. Angels will assume the shape or form with which you feel most comfortable.

Bob: But how are angels really, then?

Philip: We are beings of energy, beings of light, we can say.

Bob: Of a definite form?

Philip: Not in the sense you mean it, my friend, but rather as a form of vibration, as an energy being.

Bob: Right, thank you. Do angels think, like human beings?

Philip: No, we do not think as you do, but nonetheless we have thoughts. The thoughts are given us by higher beings, and we can then pass these on to you also.

Bob: But Philip, if you and I are talking right now, then I am receiving your thoughts and you are receiving mine – telepathically – yes?

Philip: Yes, this is true, my friend, but nonetheless I do not think in the same way as you do. My thoughts are given to me by higher beings.

Bob: So, does that mean that when we are conversing, as now, that other, higher beings are also involved in this?

Philip: Yes, it does, my friend. Remember that in the higher worlds there is not the separation that you experience in the physical world. In our worlds, beings interpenetrate each other.

Bob: So, Philip, when I communicate with you as my angel, is this different from when I'm speaking with my spirit guides, as discarnate human beings?

Philip: Yes, in a way it is, because human souls have a similar constitution, may I say. Whereas angels are not human beings, and therefore are constituted differently.

Bob: Right, Philip, thank you for that. Do angels have feelings and emotions as we do?

Philip: No, not as you do, but we do experience feelings and sensations, joy and sorrow. However, it is not the same as you know on earth.

Bob: So, how does this differ?

Philip: It is more subtle, we would say, finer in texture and tone.

Bob: Nonetheless, you do know joy and sorrow?

Philip: Yes, we do, but as I say, not in the same way as with human beings.

Bob: And what about free will, and making decisions and choices?

Philip: This we definitely do not have as you do. Human beings are unique in the universe in their gift of free will.

Bob: So, do you as angels solely follow the will of the divine?

Philip: Yes, we do. This is the will which we follow and which we serve.

Bob: Do you, as guardian angels, also work together with other sorts of angels? Let's say, angels of healing, for example?

Philip: Yes, my friend and brother, we cooperate with angels on many levels and work together with them. However, our central task is as guardian spirits of our human beings.

Bob: Do you experience joy whenever the human being in your care listens to your guidance or advice?

Philip: Indeed, we do, but very often the advice goes unheeded, unfortunately.

Bob: And is that then a cause for sorrow?

Philip: Yes, it can be. However, as I have said before, we do not experience emotions in the same way as you do as human beings. It is faithfulness and service that are our abiding characteristics.

Bob: But, if a human being acknowledges his or her angel consciously, this is recognized by the angel?

Philip: It is indeed, my friend, and this is then a source of joy, of pure joy, for us. However, even when there is no such acknowledgement, we do not cease from our task in any way.

Bob: So, it is true to describe our angel as our faithful and constant companion, our friend?

Philip: Yes, it is. We are indeed your friends, in the best sense of that earthly word. We will do everything in our power to help you fulfil your chosen destinies.

Bob: Well, Philip, I think with that in mind, we will draw this question-and-answer chapter to a close. Thank you once again.

Philip: Thank you, my friend and brother. May our work together help others to find their connections to their own angels. God bless, Philip.

Bob: Actually, Philip, just one more question. Is the universe, the cosmos, filled with beings, or is it devoid of life?

Philip: It is indeed filled with beings, with the choirs of the angels of all ranks, singing in unison and harmony to the glory of God. Yes, the universe is life-filled in every direction of the compass.

Bob: Thank you, Philip.

The Christ

Our guardian angels form part of the various angelic hierarchies. There are said to be nine such ranks of angels, stretching up to the cherubim and seraphim. We could say that, whereas the latter are the closest to the throne of God, our own angels are the closest to the human realm. As we have seen in the foregoing chapters, our guardian angels have a very specific function in relation to us human beings. They watch over us, are protective, and they try to keep us on course with our pre-birth intentions and goals for each of our incarnations. Our angels are there for us both day and night, before our birth and after death. They are our close spiritual friends and companions.

Our purpose in this section of the book has been to explore how we can obtain a much more conscious relationship to our own angel. In a sense, we can also say that our angel represents something of our own true spiritual nature, our higher self, in contrast to our ordinary, everyday personality. We are all, at core, spiritual beings clothed in earthly bodies of flesh and blood whilst incarnated on earth. When we die, our material bodies will be given back to the earth, through the processes of cremation or burial, whilst our soul and spirit begin the journey into the differentiated spheres of spirit worlds. I have discussed these things with my spirit guides and Philip in my earlier book, *Knowledge of Spirit Worlds and Life After Death*.*

How is that then with our angel and the great cosmic being whom we know as the Christ? What sort of relationship exists between them and us? It is, I think, an important question, because the Christ being, as I understand it, holds a quite unique position in regards to the whole meaning and purpose of our earthly lives. Indeed, without the intervention of the Cosmic Christ over 2,000 years ago, the positive forward evolution of humanity would be very much in question – perhaps altogether impossible. Now of course, given the dire present state of world events, with full-scale wars and the global challenge of dealing with climate change, together with many other uncertainties and upheavals,

---

* Woodward (2020).

we can certainly wonder where Christ is in all of this. If he is truly the saviour of the world, then he might well be in deep despair at where we have arrived in the twenty-first century as human beings.

However, my understanding, very much underpinned by Rudolf Steiner's anthroposophy, is that the Christ is with us today, whether we recognize him or not. In that sense, like our angel, he is always available to help and guide us through the many challenges we face, both individually and collectively. Nonetheless, and again in common with our guardian angels, Christ respects our free will and does not seek to impose himself upon us. Rather, it is up to us to freely turn towards him – to raise our sights – in order to experience his presence.

Having said that, it is, I think, much more of an inner awareness that is called for here, such as we have already described in relation to our angels. Also, like them, Christ can enable us to have a stronger sense of the true meaning and value of our earthly lives. Now, in order to avert any misunderstandings, the cosmic being that I am referring to here belongs to humanity as a whole, not just to those who follow the Christian religion. It is a universal divine presence, rather than something restricted to any particular religious denominations or Churches. Christ, in that sense, is beyond religions *per se*. Or, to put it another way, a person who considers themselves a Buddhist, Hindu, Muslim, and so on – by virtue of tradition, culture or faith – can still find a direct relationship to the inner Christ, just as they can to their angels.

Perhaps, on a quite personal note, I can refer here to a meditative verse, which was given to me by a concerned friend when I was in my 20s and struggling to find my way in life. It reads as follows,

> In the beginning was Christ,
> And Christ was with the Gods,
> And a God was Christ.
> Deep in each human soul
> Being of Christ indwells.
> In my soul too He dwells,
> And He will lead me
> To the true meaning of my life.*

---

* Rudolf Steiner (1972), p. 161.

This meditation, given by Rudolf Steiner, points to our inner soul connection with the Being of Christ. The Christ is therefore not exclusive, but is entirely inclusive of humanity as a whole. His death, resurrection and ongoing presence belong to the whole world with which he has, as I understand it, united his very being. So, having written this much by way of my introduction to this chapter, I want to now ask Philip if he can enlighten us further about all this. In particular, his relationship as an angel to the Christ Being.

Bob: Well, Philip, how do you as an angel relate to the Christ?

Philip: My friend and brother, the Christ is the being of luminous light and love whose radiance illuminates the whole of the angelic world. He is the one to whom we look up to as a shining example of service to humanity. Therefore, as an angel, I bow my head in the presence of the Christ Being, and seek to follow the example that he has set for us all.

Bob: And how does Christ support you in your task as a guardian angel?

Philip: My friend and brother, the Christ's light irradiates us and gives us strength and courage to perform the task set before us as guardian angels.

Bob: So, do you and the Christ somehow work together in supporting, guiding and helping human beings?

Philip: Yes, we do. We follow our preordained plan to help our human charges stay on track with their destinies, and the Christ in turn supports us in doing this.

Bob: So, if we manage to make a more conscious link with our angels, does this also help us to find our way to Christ?

Philip: Yes, Bob, it does. Through us, human beings can indeed open themselves to find the saviour who lives within them, and has done since the first Easter took place. He is ever present and ever available to those who turn towards him, deep in their own hearts and souls.

Bob: Many people, Philip, might find it more difficult today to relate themselves to Christ than they would to their own angel. There are many books nowadays that purport to describe people's angel experiences.

Philip: Yes, my friend, we understand what you mean and that is the reason, we can say, why the Christ also appears to many in the form or guise of an angel. He is far superior, spiritually speaking, to the angels, but he can take that form to make himself more accessible to human beings.

Bob: Well, Philip, I have read in Steiner's writings that the so-called 'Etheric Christ' can indeed appear as an angel. Correct?

Philip: Yes, he can appear among us and show himself inwardly to human beings who are open to such perceptions.

Bob: So, if I understand this correctly, the Christ can appear both in etheric form and also on a soul level within us?

Philip: Yes, correct again. He can take, and does take, both these forms of revelation.

Bob: In terms of the purpose of this book, can knowledge of the Christ also help us to build the bridge to our angels consciously?

Philip: Yes indeed, my friend. It works both ways, whether one starts with the angel or one turns towards the Christ. On both counts the pathway leads to the same inner certainty and strength for life.

Bob: And when I think of the difficulties and challenges with which we are faced nowadays, both personally and collectively, we really do need all the help we can get. Don't you agree, Philip?

Philip: I agree entirely, my friend and brother. 'Ask and you will receive' remains as relevant now as it was 2,000 years ago, when the teaching was first given.

Bob: And perhaps, Philip, with that in mind, we should bring this chapter to a close?

Philip: On the note of the importance of 'asking' for what you need, we can indeed bring our conversation to an end – for now at least. All blessings, Philip.

Bob: Thank you.

Conclusion to Part II

It is around 200 years ago that the English, London-born poet, painter and visionary, William Blake, lived and died. In his own time, he was often misunderstood, not least for his allusions to his frequent spiritual perceptions. His experience of the Archangel Gabriel was quoted at the beginning of this section. Blake is often also referred to as a prophet as well as a visionary.

In our own time there is an openness to angel experiences and to an eclectic form of spirituality not restricted by religious traditions or narrow doctrines. Many people, I suspect, do search for a deeper meaning and a sense for the riddles and challenges in their own lives. Very often, it is in times of crisis and despair, when the world seems to come tumbling down on top of us, that we seek for inner guidance and reassurance. We live also in a time where there is a greater reliance on technology and all manner of dazzling innovations.

While there may be many blessings as a result of electronic information and communication, of access to the Internet and the World Wide Web, there is also a great need for truly human interactions and connections. In fact, as many of us know only too well, our modern smartphones can cut right across the human interface and separate us, even when sitting together in the same room! It actually requires a very conscious effort today to communicate openly and directly with our fellow human beings. In some ways, we live in a modern tech-world full of contradictions and potential pitfalls, not least in building up and appreciating real human contact and dialogue.

Given this scenario, how much more challenging it may seem to build the link consciously with our angels. And yet it can be done. It is perfectly possible, if we choose to do it. As I said above, the short chapters of this book can serve as 'doorways' for linking up with our angels. They are there for us, each one of us, and when we decide to reach out to them, they will undoubtedly reciprocate in kind. To connect to our guardian angel can also open the door to a new perception of ourselves – who we really are as spiritual, human beings – the 'human form divine', in the words of William Blake.

This is important, because otherwise we may come to believe that we are nothing more than physical, material beings living on a small planet in a vast, uncaring and inhospitable universe. According to Philip, this is very far from the truth. Rather, we are very much cared for in the cosmos, which is populated by spirit beings who look to us as the creation of the gods, imbued uniquely with free will and the capacity to love. These sacred gifts have been bestowed on us in order that we can play our part in the evolution of the whole cosmos. The cosmos needs what human beings can bring to it. Therefore, the deeds of Christ on Golgotha were performed so that human beings would be able to make their future potentials available to all the company of heaven – including our own guardian angels.

In a course of lectures given in Vienna in 1914, Rudolf Steiner says an extraordinary thing when he refers to humanity as constituting 'the religion of the gods'. I will quote the relevant passage below.

> While we perceive the world, while we think in the world, feel in it, will in it, while we store up memories in order to lead a connected existence in physical life – behind all this, behind our conscious life, divine-spiritual beings are working, guiding onwards the stream of time. They have released us into space in order that there we may have as much consciousness as they deem it well for us to have, while behind this consciousness they are striving to guide our destiny further towards the great Ideal Humanity, towards the ideal of the 'religion of the gods'.*

They have, therefore, put a great deal of faith in us, and it is, I think, beholden on us to live up to their hopes and aspirations. To begin to work with our angels is one way to make this hope into a reality.

When I lived in a Camphill Community with children with special needs, we began each day before breakfast, and then also closed it after supper, with speaking certain verses together whilst standing in a circle – both children and co-workers. The evening verse was dedicated to 'the guardian angel'. Remembering this now, I realize just how important it was for us to take these words with us before entering – later – into sleep. They are:

> Thou angel of God who has charge of me,
> From the dear Father of mercifulness,

---

* Rudolf Steiner, *The Inner Nature of Man and the Life Between Death and a New Birth*, Lecture 2, Rudolf Steiner Press (2013).

The shepherding kind of the fold of the saints,
To make round about me this night.

Be thou a bright flame before me,
Be thou a guiding star above me,
Be thou a smooth path below me,
And be a kindly shepherd behind me,
Today, tonight and forever.

I am tired and I a stranger,
Lead thou me to the land of angels;
For me it is time to go home
To the court of Christ,
To the peace of heaven.*

These are the three verses which we spoke together to have this 'angel-consciousness'. Looking back, I feel very grateful that this was part of my life spent with others.

In conclusion, there is one other important thing to mention. Namely, the need to exercise a good, healthy sense of humour! Especially in relationship to ourselves, humour helps us to remain 'light', and not to take ourselves too seriously. In a recent conversation with my guardian angel, he said:

Philip: In a sense, humour is also related to joy, to a feeling of joyfulness, and the hierarchies do know of this. They experience joy in creating what God requires of them, and this puts them in good humour, we can say. Yes, we are not saying that the higher beings are filled with laughter as such –but humour, joy, they do know!

Bob: Well Philip, I've learned something that I've never thought to ask before. The humour of the gods, no less?

Philip: Yes, that's a very good way of putting it, Bob.

So with that in mind too, we can work with our angels.

---

* From *The Sun Dances: Prayers and Blessings From the Gaelic*, collected and translated by Alexander Carmichael, Christian Community Press (1966).

Addendum

My good friend Michael Allen, knowing I was in the process of writing this book, sent me a list of questions with regard to angels. Although most of these queries have already been answered in the course of the chapters, I will put them once again to Philip here. The questions are thus Michael's, but the answers are from Philip.

What are angels?

Philip: Angels, my friend and brother, are beings of light who live in the fifth dimension of existence. That is to say, in the spiritual worlds.

Where do they come from?

Philip: We come from God. He is the creator of the universe, and he has created us.

What is their relationship to us? Do we have a karmic connection to them, perhaps when they were at the human stage and we at the animal stage of development?

Philip: Our relationship to you is one of trust and protection. We are united with each one of you through being given to you by God. It is our karma to remain with you until such time that you have developed yourself spiritually, and no longer need our protection or help.

Why are angels attached to us in the role of guardians?

Philip: We are attached to you because God has seen fit to assign us to you for your good.

Is this a reciprocal arrangement? Do guardian angels get anything from us?

Philip: Yes, we do also receive from you, because through your love, we too are able to take a step up in our own development.

I have read that the adversarial beings feed on our fears. Could it be that guardian angels feed on our positive thoughts and emotions?

Philip: Yes, we do feed on your positive thoughts, emotions, and especially your love. These enable us to draw close to you.

It is said by some that angels are situated behind us. Is that true, and if so, why is this?

Philip: It is true that we often stand behind you in order to give you our protection. However, depending on the circumstances, we can also be at your side, or even in front of you if need be.

Do guardian angels have more than one human in their charge? Do they live very different lives in much expanded dimensions of their consciousness, apart from their role of concentrating on us as our guardians?

Philip: No, we do not have charge of more than one human being. This is the person who has been given into our care. As guardian angels, our focus is very much on our human charges, and therefore our lives are circumscribed in this direction and dimension.

Do angels have free will? I have read that only human beings have this, tied with the capacity for love. If angels don't have free will, how could Lucifer have rebelled?

Philip: No, we do not have free will. This is a gift that is bestowed on human beings only. Lucifer was able to rebel because God allowed him to do so, so that human beings could evolve their freedom.

Most people don't know about guardian angels. Therefore, how and in what manner is it possible for our guardian angels to help in these cases? Such people would not know to ask the guardian angel for help, as they don't even know they have a guardian angel. As the beings who work for the light are meant to respect our free will, would it be true that people's ignorance in this respect would hinder the angels work greatly?

Philip: Whether people recognize us or not, it is our mission to help them in all ways that we can. If people acknowledge us and work with us, then we are enabled to help them more than might otherwise be possible.

Do guardian angels follow us through the gates of death and into a new incarnation?

Philip: Yes, we do. We never abandon you, but accompany you through life on earth and your lives in spirit worlds also. And then, of course, also into your new incarnations on earth.

Bob: Right, Philip, thank you for answering Michael's questions.

PART III

NINE CONVERSATIONS WITH CHRIST

Introduction to Part III

I am writing this note on the day after Christmas day, 2022. In other words, on the second of the twelve days of Christmastide. It was on this very day that I had a highly original thought, one that I have never had before. Namely, to see if it is possible for me to have conscious, telepathic conversations with the Christ. I do mean precisely the Christ Being, rather than the Master Jesus or *Sananda*, as he is sometimes referred to.

For nearly 18 years I have been having inner telepathic conversations with my spirit guides, i.e., with discarnate human beings living in spirit worlds. Similarly, I have also conversed with my guardian angel, Philip, using the same methodology. It is on the basis of this work, which bridges the threshold between the sensory and supersensible worlds, that I now dare to wonder if I might also be permitted to enter into dialogue with the living Christ.

In a collection of lectures, mostly given in 1910 by Rudolf Steiner (1861–1925), the founder of anthroposophy, we can read about the nature of the so-called 'Second Coming'. The etheric is the sphere of the life-forces that underpin all the various lifeforms on earth, and it is also that realm in which the Christ can today manifest 'outwardly' to us human beings. According to Steiner, the Christ will not appear again in an actual physical, material body, as he did 2,000 or so years ago in the Holy Land. But he can and does take on an etheric sheath. In this way, he can appear to us as if he is really a physical person, though in fact he is not.

Steiner gives us an impressive description of this as follows:

> Individuals may become aware that someone has suddenly approached to help them become alert to something. The truth is, Christ has come to them, although they believe that they see a physical man. They will come to realize, however, that this is a suprasensory being, since he will immediately vanish. Many will have this experience while sitting silently in a room, oppressed with a heavy heart and not knowing which way to turn. The door will open, and the Etheric Christ

will appear to console that person. The Christ will become a living comforter. Though it may seem strange now, it is nevertheless true that even large numbers of people will often be sitting together and wondering what to do, and they will see the Etheric Christ. He will be there and confer with them; he will cast his word into such gatherings.*

To fully appreciate this new appearance of the Christ, it is good to study the whole collection of lectures referred to above.

If we take it quite literally, that Christ can become a living counsellor to us incarnated human beings, I feel that I may perhaps be allowed to address myself to him directly, to ask for his counsel and advice. However, my motive for doing this is certainly not for myself alone. Rather, it is so that I may perform some service to my fellow men and women by showing that he is indeed available to us all in our modern day and age.

Therefore, the following conversations, if indeed they will happen, are intended with that very specific purpose in mind. Namely, to help make more people aware of this new reality, this new presence, in our midst. Just as we may call upon our own guardian angel, or else our own spirit guides, to ask for their help and advice, so, if I understand it rightly, we may call upon the Christ. This is a really quite amazing and uplifting thought; a thought that can fill us with wonder, humility and gratitude! To earnestly explore this possibility during the blessed time of Christmas and the Holy Nights seems to me very appropriate.

I will, therefore, in all humility, address myself to him and see what I may receive telepathically in return, and share this content with you. I look forward to doing this at those times in the coming days when I can sit, in the right frame of heart and mind, to transmit his thoughts, for us then to contemplate and think upon. Just as I need to be in the right mood of soul to do this spiritual work, so you, as reader, would need to be receptive in the best way you can to whatever is given in the pages that follow.

However, I am not asking anyone to simply believe and accept what is written here. We are thinking beings, and it is right to exercise that divine gift to form our own views. To do that, we need to take

___
* Rudolf Steiner, *The Reappearance of Christ in the Etheric* (2003), p. xiii.

care to recognize our own prejudices and preconceived notions. Only by doing so can we hope to be open-minded and open-hearted. Also, to consider that – whether or not we aspire to a Christian faith – we may be able to discover our own personal inner relationship to this unique being.

Perhaps this meditative verse, given by Rudolf Steiner, can help us to be ready to receive what is to be shared in this book?

It reads:

> In the Beginning was Christ,
> And Christ was with the Gods,
> And a God was Christ.
> Deep in each human soul
> Being of Christ indwells.
> In my soul too He dwells,
> And He will lead me
> To the true meaning of my life.

These words are contained in the book *Verses and Meditations** by Rudolf Steiner. Actually, the last such entry in this volume also impressively reads:

> Christ knows us. To a soul that sees our spiritual science in the true light, to a heart that feels it in its true significance, I can impart no more esoteric saying: *The Christ is seeing us.*[†]

Whilst the above was said by Steiner in 1915 to persons probably very familiar with his anthroposophy, or spiritual science, nonetheless, it is impressive to hear of the nearness of the Christ, of his knowing and seeing such souls. Therefore, to enter into genuine conversations with the Christ will, I think, also call upon our own openness of heart as well as our mind. In that sense, we may speak of a real 'Christ-mass' event at any time in our individual lives, as an experience of the sacred.

I do of course realize that for some people it may appear audacious and stretching the bounds of credulity that I have agreed to the publishing of such conversations. However, I have done so because I am very clear about my inner motivations and intentions. I'm not in the least

---

* R. Steiner, *Verses and Meditations* (1972), p. 161.
[†] Ibid., p., 223.

interested to draw attention to myself, but only to confirm the reality of Christ's continual presence in our midst. This is, I believe, important for us to know about, and for us to have ready access to in our times of greatest need – or even in normal, everyday life. He walks with us and our destiny continually.

All blessings
Bob

First Conversation

Prologue

So, as I sit at my bureau this evening, I am ready now to address my question to the Christ. This is something that I have not done before in this way, though of course there have certainly been moments in my life when, in some desperation, I have asked for his help. Now, as I sit here in expectation, I am not in desperate straits, but I do wish to converse with him who has united himself with humanity.

Conversation

Bob: Dear Christ, may I speak with you?

Christ: Yes, my son, you can indeed speak with me, and I with you. Tell me what it is that you wish from me.

Bob: I wish, in the first place, to confirm that you are who you say you are. How can I be sure that I am really in touch with you?

Christ: You can be sure of this, my son, because you know how to converse with those in spirit worlds. Therefore, you also know how to converse with me, and you know in your heart of hearts that I will never deceive you or claim to be someone who I am not. Therefore, know that I am indeed the being whom you and others refer to as 'the Christ'. Namely, the Son of God and the one who has direct access to the Father, because the Father lives in me and I live in the Father. This is who I am.

Bob: Thank you. My understanding, largely gleaned from the works of Rudolf Steiner, is that you can be with us in our times of need, that you are able to make your presence known, and even to *appear* to those who are in need. Am I correct in this?

Christ: Yes, my son, you are correct in all that you say. I am there for whoever needs me. Whenever someone is in need and calls upon me, I will respond and answer their call.

Bob: Yes, I have on occasions certainly asked for your help, O Christ, but I have not seen you appear in front of me. Can you give help without necessarily showing yourself?

Christ: Yes indeed, my son, I can do so. It is not always necessary for me to appear in front of someone in order for me to be there for them. In some cases, it would be too shocking for a person to suddenly see me there in front of them. Therefore, I give help in the best way that I can, depending on the particular circumstances.

Bob: When Rudolf Steiner describes your reappearance in the etheric realm, is that true?

Christ: Yes, my son, it is true, but as I have said, it is not always necessary or appropriate.

Bob: How then do you decide, if I can put it like that, whether it is appropriate or not?

Christ: It is appropriate when it is helpful. When it gives added assurance – added proof, you could say – that I am there to help the person in pain or sorrow or need. This is something that I can judge by seeing the state of soul of the person in question. If I know it will help that person to see me, then I will appear before them.

Bob: But why do so at all? Why is it that in our modern times – I mean since the 1940s, according to Rudolf Steiner – that you would appear at all? Why is it necessary?

Christ: It is necessary, my son, because many people require proof. Seeing is believing in the age in which you live. Therefore, to further that belief and that seeing, I come in the form that gives the assurance that is needed.

Bob: I can imagine that it could give a huge amount of reassurance and comfort to some people?

Christ: Indeed, it does, and therefore I am only too happy to be able to give what is needed in this way.

Bob: If I asked to see you, would you show yourself to me?

Christ: If you ask for this then I will certainly do so. However, you will need to be alert for my appearance, because I may not take the form which you might expect.

Bob: Well, I would indeed ask you to show me yourself in whatever way that you can, before I finish the conversations that I have with you.

Christ: This I will do. Be alert and awake, and I will show myself to you. Perhaps when you least expect it.

Bob: Right. I will do my best to be awake for that experience. Thank you. I would like to ask that you perhaps guide me, O Christ, in our conversations, because I want them to be of benefit to others – to those who choose to read this book. Therefore, I ask for your guidance as to the contents that should flow to them. Is that all right?

Christ: It is all right, my son. I will give guidance as to what you will ask of me, so that your work will serve the needs of others.

Bob: Thank you. I feel that we have made a beginning, and as it is not far off midnight, I will draw this first dialogue to a close. I thank you again for responding to me, telepathically, in the same way that I am used to talking to friends in spirit.

Christ: Yes, my son, I have made use of your gifts to bring through my answers to your questions. And I will do this likewise when you turn to me again and ask for my counsel. God's blessing be with you, and my peace also.

Bob: Thank you.

Note: However incredible this may all sound, I can only say that I received these communications in exactly the same way as I have with my guides over the past 18 years. Therefore, I put my trust in their authenticity.

Second Conversation

Prologue

Once again, I am sat in my room. I have just read the first conversation, received yesterday, and I will ask to resume dialogue with the Christ this evening, now. May I do this in the right mood of soul, knowing that I wish to be of help to others by doing so.

Conversation

Bob: O Christ, may I speak with you again this evening?

Christ: Yes, my son, you may, and I will respond to you. Ask me what you wish to know and I will answer you.

Bob: Was it really necessary that you died on the cross on Golgotha? Could there have been a different way to achieve your mission, your aims?

Christ: No, my son there was no other way but to go through the pain of death. Only by doing this, could I accomplish my deed for all humanity. There was no other way to achieve the goal, the mission, that had been given to me by the Father. Only thus could I be the force for resurrection and rejuvenation of the earth and of humanity upon the earth.

Bob: But this was a terrible death to go through. Surely, bad enough for an ordinary human being to endure, but far worse for a god?

Christ: Yes, far worse for a god. And yet, out of this suffering was born the force of redemption for mankind.

Bob: Is it true that the other gods – the spiritual beings in the spirit worlds – know nothing of death?

Christ: Yes, it is true. Death such as you know it on earth was unknown to all the gods. Therefore, it was necessary that a god would go through this human experience.

Bob: And did you then tell the others in spirit how that was?

Christ: Yes, they learnt of death through me. But they learnt of the power of redemption and resurrection through me also. Therefore, my mission on earth was completed, and will be fully completed in the times to come.

Bob: Did the disciples understand what had happened to you?

Christ: No, they did not. Only when they saw me again and listened to the teachings I gave them did they begin to understand what had taken place through me.

Bob: And I wonder, O Christ, how many modern people in our own time understand what you did and who you are?

Christ: Not many, I can assure you. And I pray that very many more will come to me, will realize that I live in them, and that they can understand the meaning of my life for them

Bob: Rudolf Steiner has tried, in his anthroposophy, to make you and your deeds understandable to others.

Christ: Yes, he was indeed a servant of the Light and he has endeavoured to spread the word of understanding to those who have ears to hear.

Bob: Is it true, O Christ, that more and more people will be able to have a personal experience of your presence in their lives?

Christ: Yes, this is true. I will make myself known to all those who seek me and are receptive to my presence.

Bob: Does it matter if such people are Christians or belong to other religions or faiths?

Christ: No, it makes no difference to me. All are human beings, and it is to the human being that I make myself known and available to all.

Bob: O Christ, I think I had better get some sleep. Hopefully, better than I managed last night.

Christ: Yes, get some sleep and rest assured that you are watched over and cared for by me and by the angels. God's blessing be with you, and my peace.

Bob: Thank you, O Christ.

Note: The conversations are short. It is only possible for me to maintain that right mood of soul for so long. So, rather 'short and sweet' than prolonged, I would say.

Third Conversation

Bob: O Christ, may I once again return to you this evening, so that we can come into conversation?

Christ: Yes, my son, you can. Ask me what it is you wish to know.

Bob: It is said, O Christ, that you live deep in each human soul. Is this true?

Christ: It is indeed true. I live in the depth of your soul, and in the soul of every human being. It remains, however, in your freedom as to whether I am recognized in the soul.

Bob: Well, I ponder on the words, 'Christ in me'. How can I make these words more real? How can I experience *you*?

Christ: You can experience me in your heart. It is in your heart that you will feel my presence, when you turn there with humility and with expectation.

Bob: Is it these feelings that help us to give birth to this knowledge, this recognition within ourselves?

Christ: Yes, it is. When you sit quietly and come to peace in yourself, then you will experience me living in your heart, in your soul.

Bob: But many people seem to be totally distracted by everything around them. I wonder how often they bring themselves to stillness, let alone peace?

Christ: What you say is true, my son, but when they really need me, I will be there for them, and they will experience this if their hearts are not closed.

Bob: So, is it true to say, O Christ, that you can make your presence known to us in two ways, two directions, so to speak? I mean inwardly, but also sometimes outwardly in your etheric form?

Christ: Yes, both ways are possible – from within and from without.

Bob: Could it be that when some people think or feel that an angel has come close to help them, that actually that angel is you?

Christ: Yes, this does happen. It may also be that it is their own angel who has come to them, but it can also be me that has been mistaken for an angel. Either way, they will then feel supported and helped in their time of need.

Bob: I have also read that you can actually appear 'etherically', and speak words of comfort and consolation. Is that also true?

Christ: Yes, it is true. I can appear and I can speak to those who need advice, counsel or guidance.

Bob: So, are you everywhere?

Christ: I am everywhere. There is nowhere where I am not.

Bob: So, it doesn't matter where a particular person is living on the earth geographically? You can still be with them?

Christ: I can, and I am.

Bob: But what if several people all need you at the same time, or maybe a hundred or a thousand people, all in that same moment? What then?

Christ: Then I will be with each one of them, because I am *in* each one of them. I am not bounded by time or space as you understand them, my son.

Bob: Can you also heal people if they ask for your help? You will know that I do this for certain people – to ask you, that is.

Christ: I can help to the extent that karma and freedom let me help. I do not transgress either karma or a person's inner freedom.

Bob: So, do you mean that you will do all you can to help within these parameters?

Christ: Yes, I do. I will help if I am able to help, in every way that I can.

Bob: When you lived on earth in Jesus, you often said, I think, that, 'Your faith has healed you' (or 'made you whole'), when asked to help a sick person. Is that right?

Christ: That is correct. I called upon their own faith to bring about the healing that was needed.

Bob: So, was this a self-healing process?

Christ: Yes, it was. The person in question released their own forces for healing their ills through their faith and belief.

Bob: So, it wasn't you who did the healing?

Christ: I have never done the healing. Healing comes to me from my Father. I have never done healing out of myself alone. The Father and I are at one.

Bob: But with the Father, you can help heal us?

Christ: With the Father, all things are possible.

Bob: But you have taken away the sins of the world, have you not?

Christ: I have cleansed the earth, Mother Earth, of the effects of all the sins that human beings have committed on her from time immemorial. Yes, that I have done, through the grace of the Father.

Bob: But we, each of us, still has to bear our own karma and bring this into balance?

Christ: Yes, you do. Each one is responsible for their own actions, and must bear the consequences of their deeds. The earth is freed from sin through me, but each human being must carry their own destiny.

Bob: Are you with us, O Christ, as you said, until the end of the world?

Christ: I am with you until the end of the world.

Bob: I think I should finish this now, though our conversation indeed flowed very easily. Thank you for being with me.

Christ: I am with you always. May God's blessing be with you, and my peace.

Bob: Thank you.

Fourth Conversation

Prologue

It is New Year's Eve 2022/23, and I am sat again at my bureau. I will see if I can have another conversation with Christ.

Conversation

Bob: O Christ, may I again converse with you, not for my sake, but for the sake of all those who will read my planned book and gain reassurance from it?

Christ: Yes, my son, let us speak again together and then share this conversation with all who wish to partake in it.

Bob: O Christ, why did you come to live on the earth?

Christ: I came to live on the earth because my Father wished me to come here to help the human beings who live on this planet. The Father sent me, and I willingly followed his wish.

Bob: But why did he send you?

Christ: He sent me to redeem the earth and to redeem humanity from their sins and transgressions.

Bob: And why did humanity create this sin, this sin which the earth suffered?

Christ: They were led astray by Lucifer, who had fallen away from his heavenly role and who defied the Father.

Bob: And why did Lucifer do this?

Christ: In order to give human beings their freedom – their inner freedom.

Bob: But then surely the Father allowed this to happen?

Christ: Yes, my Father allowed Lucifer to fall from grace, so that he could bestow freedom on human souls.

Bob: So, Lucifer's falling was also part of God's plan for mankind? For mankind's evolution?

Christ: Yes, it was. Nothing is possible without the Father's agreement. So yes, it was part of the plan of creation.

Bob: Who is the Father, your Father?

Christ: He is the Godhead, the supreme creator of the universe, the cosmos.

Bob: And what of the Trinity, of Father, Son and Holy Spirit?

Christ: Yes, we are three and we are one.

Bob: So, are you, O Christ, equal with the Father?

Christ: I am equal with the Father, because the Father is in me and I am in the Father. We are one.

Bob: And yet you can be there, here, for each single human being?

Christ: Yes, I live in each human soul.

Bob: Even if they have no awareness, no knowledge of you? Even if they belong to different religious faiths than Christianity?

Christ: Yes, I belong to all human beings, whatever their faiths, beliefs or knowledge.

Bob: And how can they – we, I – find you?

Christ: Look into your own heart. Be still and look within, and you will find me.

Bob: But are we not unworthy, totally unworthy, of your love and presence, O Christ?

Christ: No, you are not. You are children of God, and God loves each one of you, as he also loves me.

Bob: And yet, we are selfish and self-centred. And human beings do terrible things to others, be they people, animals, plants, or even the solid earth. How can you, or God, love us?

Christ: We love you unconditionally, because you are part of God's creation. He has set you upon the earth and he loves each one of you.

Bob: Well, I must of course accept what you say, though some people have strayed very far from their divine origin. Not so?

Christ: Yes, some have. But, however far they have strayed, they can be brought back into the fold – into the sheepfold – because I am the Shepherd of the sheep.

Bob: Well then, we should all be filled with hope for the future, in spite of all that has happened and is happening on earth.

Christ: Yes, hope for the future is always there. We must see how long it takes for each of my sheep to come back to the sheepfold.

Bob: Maybe for some, that will take a very long time?

Christ: Yes, it may indeed. But I am here until the end of the world.

Bob: And how long is that?

Christ: It is longer than time as you know it now. It is beyond time.

Bob: O Christ, what must we do to draw near to you?

Christ: Love one another as I have loved you. When you do this, then I am with you.

Bob: But what of those who hate, despise or fear their fellows? Are you far from them?

Christ: No, I am not far from them, but they are far from me.

Bob: How so?

Christ: Because they do not draw near to me, even though I live deep in their souls.

Bob: So, love is really the thing – the bridge, the key – to find you?

Christ: My love is in them. Their love must find me.

Bob: When I think of humanity right now, and also the state of the world due largely to our behaviours, it really doesn't look good. Can we make things better?

Christ: You can always make things better than they are today, but to do so requires love, action, courage and will. With these, you can help to make the world better.

Bob: Well, O Christ, the Christmas message is, 'Peace to men on earth in whom lives goodwill'. But there is still no peace on earth, and not enough goodwill.

Christ: What you say is true, but my peace is there for anyone who turns to me and fills himself with my love and peace. With me.

Bob: Well, I can only hope that more and more people will come to you, O Christ, including myself.

Christ: You have already come to me, my son. Therefore, you can speak with me now. I hope that many more will come to me, so that I can fill them with my peace.

Bob: Yes, so do I. Why is there such a thing as evil?

Christ: Evil is there so that the greatest good can come about. Without evil there can be no good.

Bob: So, are you saying that evil beings are there to serve the good? Is that what you're saying?

Christ: Yes, that is what I'm saying. All evil beings ultimately serve the good, and all will be redeemed by this same good.

Bob: I think somewhere in the Gospels, when someone referred to you as 'the good master', you said: 'Why call me good? Only God is good.' Am I right with this?

Christ: Yes, you are right with this. Only God is good. All other beings can become good by becoming one with God. All evil beings strive to become good also when they turn to God, who is their creator.

Bob: So, are you saying that God has created the so-called evil beings?

Christ: God has created all beings, including those you choose to call evil.

Bob: Do you mean that they are not really evil?

Christ: No beings are truly evil, but they must play this role for the sake of God's plan for creation. Without evil there cannot come about the greatest good for human beings.

Bob: So, is all this for the benefit, the sake, of humanity?

Christ: Yes, it is. For humanity's sake God has allowed evil to appear in the world. Through its transformation the greatest good will be manifest.

Bob: Well, there is no doubt that much evil has been done by human beings upon their fellows. Not so?

Christ: It is so, indeed. Much harm, much suffering, much evil, has been done at the hands of human beings. But all will be redeemed in time, and beyond time.

Bob: Well, thank God for that!

Christ: Thank God indeed.

Bob: I think on this note I will bring this conversation to an end, O Christ. I thank you for allowing me to speak with you.

Christ: I thank you, my son, for being willing to hear my voice. May God's blessing be with you, and my peace also.

Bob: Thank you.

Fifth Conversation

Prologue

I hope this evening, on New Year's Day 2023, to turn again to the Christ Being and to speak with him on important matters. Of course, I know that there will be people, perhaps the majority, who think that I'm deluding myself; that there is no way we ordinary people can communicate with the Christ. Maybe at the holy altar the ordained priests can be our interlocutors for him, but certainly not you or I. But then, it wouldn't be true to say, 'Christ lives in us', in each one of us, as he himself claims.

If indeed he *does* live in us, in our souls, then everyone has access to him, if they earnestly turn towards him. This is all that I'm doing – nothing more or less. I turn to the living Christ in my heart and soul and speak with him, as I would anyone else. Why not? Why should this not be possible? Christ is our companion, our guide, our comforter, in this earthly life. We can talk to him and receive his words. This is what I believe, and I think this is exactly what I'm doing in these conversations. If others think differently, that's all right by me. I am not putting forward any dogma. But I am saying, turn to him if you wish to, and speak with him, and listen for his voice within you. Yes, I don't as such hear 'a voice', but I do receive the thoughts that flow into me. I believe these are Christ's thoughts, not mine.

Having said this I will, I hope, later today, probably in the quiet of the evening, sit again and turn to him. I look forward to this. Amen.

*

Conversation

Bob: O Christ, I wish to speak with you again. Can I do so?

Christ: Yes, you can, my son. I'm here with you, within you, and I will speak with you.

Bob: I wonder, O Christ, if I can ask you concrete questions concerning the present state of the world?

Christ: Yes, you can, and I will answer you.

Bob: Very well. At present there is this terrible war going on between Russia and Ukraine. Why is this?

Christ: The war is there because fear is there. The war is the result of fear.

Bob: Is it Russia then that fears Ukraine, or the other way around, or both?

Christ: It is both. Both fear each other, and where there is fear, there is no love. Without love, there can be no peace.

Bob: Well, there will be no love lost in these two nations, will there?

Christ: Without love between nations there is no peace, only fear, distrust and unhappiness.

Bob: Well, I'm afraid I can't imagine any way soon, or in the foreseeable future, that there will be love between Russia and Ukraine. Not after all that has happened and is happening now.

Christ: Yes, what you say is true, but only when there is love, will there be true peace.

Bob: Before this started, there may have been love, some love between the peoples of these countries. After all, I believe they are closely related by culture and geography.

Christ: Yes, they are, and there was love between these nations before the war started.

Bob: Then we must hope that what was there before can be regained?

Christ: Yes, with goodwill it can be restored.

Bob: Are there spiritual beings, adversarial beings, who have a hand in this war?

Christ: Yes, there are. Many demons are working hard to fan the flames of this conflict and destruction.

Bob: Why?

Christ: Because they seize every opportunity to sow discord and hatred between people.

Bob: Why?

Christ: Because only by doing so can they fulfil their purpose.

Bob: So, their purpose is to sow conflict?

Christ: Yes, it is, and thereby provide the opportunity for greater love, freedom and selflessness to come about.

Bob: It seems a great pity that such beings are called upon to do this. I mean to stoke the fires of fear and hatred.

Christ: Yes, on the earthly level it is like this. On the heavenly level, it is seen differently.

Bob: I suppose it's only after time has run its course that many things will become clearer, to us at least?

Christ: This is true. Only in time will it be seen why this or that earthly event has come to pass.

Bob: Can I ask you, O Christ, about the coronavirus pandemic?

Christ: Yes, you can.

Bob: Why has it come to humanity?

Christ: It has come to teach lessons. To enable you to learn how to live with each other differently. To value what is most important in your lives on earth.

Bob: And how can it do that?

Christ: By waking you up. By showing you that what you seek is not to be found in purely material terms, but in your true human relationships, as brothers and sisters.

Bob: I'm not sure I understand what you mean.

Christ: I mean that it is in the love which you show to one another that you will find the meaning in your lives. Not through pursuing purely earthly goals.

Bob: So, was this pandemic meant to be? Was it God-given?

Christ: No, it was not God-given. It was created by men and it will have to be solved by men also.

Bob: You mean that we brought this on ourselves?

Christ: Yes, you brought it on yourselves.

Bob: How?

Christ: By misusing your own capacities, and letting Nature take her revenge on you.

Bob: I'm not sure people would necessarily agree with that.

Christ: Perhaps not, nonetheless what I have said is true.

Bob: So, maybe the real way to overcome the pandemic is a change of heart, a change of attitude, rather than just giving vaccinations?

Christ: The cause must be treated, not simply the symptoms.

Bob: So, does this also have to do with our whole relationship to Nature, to the kingdoms of Nature, as human beings?

Christ: Yes, it does. You need to respect Nature in all its forms, so that Nature can truly serve you.

Bob: Instead of exploiting her?

Christ: Yes, instead of exploiting Nature for your own selfish ends.

Bob: Can Nature be restored, repaired, rejuvenated, if we give her a chance to do so?

Christ: Nature has great reserves of self-replenishment, but human beings must not prevent this from taking place.

Bob: But isn't it inevitable that Nature must change? I mean, that certain species die out and that changes take place?

Christ: Yes, in some ways it is. However, the pace of change depends very much on how humans treat Nature, with respect or abuse.

Bob: The world has become so much smaller. With modern communications and technology we can know what is happening in every part immediately.

Christ: Yes, you can, and therefore you should use this knowledge for the good of all life on the planet.

Bob: Well, if everyone had the right motives and goals, we could, I suppose. But I'm afraid we're far from reaching that ideal state.

Christ: Yes, you are. But until you reach that there will be one calamity after another. There is no other way to learn and grow.

Bob: Yes, it is pretty obvious really, isn't it?

Christ: It is, and yet humanity is slow to learn its lessons and to learn to care for one another and all life on earth.

Bob: Yes, that is indeed true. I will have further questions, but for tonight I will bring our conversation to a close. Thank you.

Christ: Thank you, my son, for once again entering into dialogue with me. Would others do likewise. God's blessing on you, and my peace.

Bob: Thank you.

Sixth Conversation

Prologue

So, once again I sit at my bureau. Actually, it was my father's bureau, which I received after he died. This evening I looked through family photograph albums, including one which my parents made for me. Such albums are full of memories. I do not often, in fact very rarely, look at these photos. But to do so, as this evening, gives overviews of lives and lifetimes. Of childhood, youth, adulthood, old age, the phases of growing up through life. It leaves me with a feeling of gratitude for all that life has given me, with our family: holidays on the Isles of Scilly, happy days to have lived through as the children grew from year to year.

No doubt, or at least I hope, many people can likewise look back on their lives, on their families. So, if now I turn to Christ, to speak with him again, then I feel I must also reflect on the mystery of our lives on earth, if in reality we are essentially spiritual beings. Perhaps we spend a longer time, maybe much longer, in our spirit lives between death and a new birth on earth? At any event, we don't remember that life, and we have no photograph albums to remind us of it. And then, if we think that we have probably had many lifetimes on planet earth, well then, that is really quite a thought – the mystery, the sense, the purpose of our earthly lives! Oh, to understand this, to fathom the mystery!

Conversation

Bob: O Christ, may I once again turn to you and speak with you?

Christ: Yes, my son, you may. Tell me what it is you wish to know.

Bob: Well, I have looked back, via photographs, on the course of my life and the lives of my children, my wife and also my parents. It is quite something to have such pictures from the past. Are not our lives on earth something of a mystery? Maybe a mystery drama?

Christ: My son, your lives on earth are a blessing, a gift from God. By them you are given the opportunities to learn, to grow, to become.

This is why you altogether *are* born into this world. This world that I'm also a part of, since the first Easter and my death and resurrection.

Bob: O Christ, I do find it an incredible thought to really imagine that we have had many lives on the earth. Lives that have spanned different cultures, languages, places and peoples. If we remembered all that, it would be too much to take in, wouldn't it?

Christ: It would indeed, and therefore God in his wisdom and love does not allow your memory to extend that far into the past. A veil of forgetfulness is wrapped around you when you enter a new birth on the earth.

Bob: Yes, I can see that this is needed if we are to really put ourselves freshly into the new lifetime, the new incarnation.

Christ: Yes, indeed, if you were not protected in this way, you would be overwhelmed by all the memories of your pasts. Therefore, divine grace allows you to enter into life with a blank space, so to speak. A *tabula rasa*.

Bob: Yes, that is certainly necessary. Yet perhaps some people also bear memories of their previous life or lives? Can that happen?

Christ: It can indeed, but in those cases, it may cause difficulties to cope with the present lifetime.

Bob: Yes, I have heard of some examples of people remembering earlier lifetimes. I don't know how well they cope with that in leading their current lives.

Christ: Well, this has to be seen individually, since each person may deal with these past events differently.

Bob: Well, in my case, O Christ, I cannot even remember much at all of my own childhood in *this* life, so I certainly am not troubled by past lifetimes. At least not consciously.

Christ: No, that is true. But it is enough to take stock of all that happens in one human life, for that indeed contains many memories and many events.

Bob: Can you tell us, O Christ, what is really the mystery of our human lives on earth? I mean, if we are really spiritual beings, then why do we incarnate at all?

Christ: You incarnate in order to transform this planet into a star. Into a shining, radiant star of love, shining out into the cosmos. This is the mystery of your human lives. You are all working on the transformation of the planet and the transformation of yourselves.

Bob: But why?

Christ: Because this is the divine plan of creation. Also, the plan of evolution towards the goal which the Father has set before you.

Bob: So, we are all part of that plan?

Christ: Yes, you are. Every human being, every human soul, is following that plan, which the Father has set in motion many aeons ago.

Bob: Is this where our own destiny comes into play?

Christ: Yes, it is. Each one of you has your destiny, which you yourselves have created. And it is on the earth that you strive to realize your destiny and progress stage by stage on your path of evolution.

Bob: And our individual destinies are joined, can I say, somehow united, with those of others in the overall plan of evolution?

Christ: Yes, they are. They work together towards the goal that the earth will be transformed, will be spiritualized more and more through the work of human beings.

Bob: But probably most people living on the earth today are totally unaware of all this?

Christ: Yes, that is true, but in time more and more people should awaken to this awareness of their greater purpose in life.

Bob: I think we have rather a way to go before such an awareness takes hold?

Christ: Yes, all things take time, but remember, I am with you until the end of the world.

Bob: Well, thank God for that, because I think we need all the help we can get.

Christ: Yes, you are right in this. However, if more and more people become aware of me living in them, then I can help them to realize the true purpose of their lives in the great plan of evolution.

Bob: Well, I hope our conversations, O Christ, may help towards such an awareness of you. It would be wonderful, I feel, if people could really relate to you *in* them.

Christ: It would indeed, and gradually this will come about, God willing.

Bob: But since we have freedom, or at least we have it potentially, each person must come to you in their own way and time. Not so?

Christ: That is true. Each person is free to turn towards me when they are ready to do so. I wait within them, for them to recognize me.

Bob: It is then a very personal matter, is it not?

Christ: Yes, it is indeed. Each person will come to this in their own time. Therefore, I must wait on this, in each one.

Bob: Perhaps I will leave our conversation at this point for tonight. Is that all right?

Christ: Yes, it is all right. It is your initiative to speak with me, my son.

Bob: Thank you.

Christ: May God's peace be with you, and mine.

Bob: I thank you for that.

Note: When I am conversing in this way, the thoughts just flow. I myself am amazed at this. I feel it to be natural, and yet I also feel that it is quite remarkable. Because the communication is by thought, the thoughts that flow to me, into me, are like mine, but not mine. I do not hear voices, but I do perceive the thoughts very clearly. To think that in such a way we can speak with the Christ is an amazing thought. Yet, why should this not be? If he is in us, each one of us, why should we not speak, inwardly, with him?

Seventh Conversation

Prologue

Once again, I am sat down and hope to enter into conversation with Christ. I have just watched a documentary programme on the television on channel 4 called *2022: The Year from Space*. It shows what could be seen from satellites situated in space looking down at our blue planet. It featured changes due to human activity, ranging from the depletion of the Amazon rainforest and the devastating war in Ukraine to natural events like hurricanes, earthquakes, migrations of animals, etc. It was fascinating to get such overviews. Two former astronauts also commented from time to time from their own observations when on-board the International Space Station. As one of them pointed out at the end of the programme, the earth is our planet and we need to take care of it – it is our home in space, for all humanity. True though this is, we shouldn't lose sight of the other parts of humanity not living at present on the earth, but in the Spirit. The totality of humanity spans both heaven and earth.

So now I will let the meditation verse, 'In the beginning was Christ... ', flow through me before speaking with him and asking some questions.

Conversation

Bob: O Christ, I turn to you once again, on the one hand knowing full well of my unworthiness and shortcomings but on the other hand recognizing that you are our inner guide, comforter and companion. May I speak with you again?

Christ: Yes, my son, you can. Please tell me what you want to know.

Bob: Well, having just watched a television programme showing the earth from space, I can only be awed by the beauty of our planet, but also appalled by how human beings often treat it. Are you not also dismayed at how we behave towards the earth, Mother Earth?

Christ: I am saddened by human abuse of the planet, yes, but I also know that if humanity would work together, then much can be saved.

Bob: Yes, I know some people, maybe many, are trying to restore health and balance to the natural world. Others, of course, take advantage of Nature for their own ends.

Christ: Yes, what you say is true. However, let us hope that the good side of humanity will shine through and restore much that has been destroyed or spoilt. The future lies very much in the hands of human beings.

Bob: I think Nature does have tremendous ability to bounce back, so to speak, if given a chance.

Christ: She does.

Bob: I would like to ask this question, O Christ. I understand that on the one hand, you live in each of us, in our souls, and on the other hand, you can also appear to us in etheric garb, as if you are a physical human being. Am I correct in this?

Christ: Yes, my son, you are absolutely right in this. I appear both inwardly and outwardly, as needs be.

Bob: How does your etheric appearance come about?

Christ: Yes, I clothe myself in the world ether and appear then to visible etheric sight. Many may mistake me then for a physical person, but I am not physical but etheric in substance.

Bob: And this is what is meant by your so-called Second Coming?

Christ: Yes, it is. It is my reappearance in the etheric realm.

Bob: Is this done to give us reassurance? Maybe to strengthen our faith and belief?

Christ: It is done to bring comfort and counsel when it is needed by suffering or troubled human souls.

Bob: What does it take to awaken people to your inner presence? To realize that you are the Christ within us?

Christ: This needs a greater awareness and a greater maturity of soul. This is not so easy for most people to realize, because they do not come to peace and stillness and listen to their own hearts.

Bob: Why is it that I can now communicate with you, O Christ?

Christ: Because you have learnt to do this inner communication, this communing, with your spiritual guides and helpers. Therefore, you can also do this with me.

Bob: But many people may find this very far-fetched and difficult to accept.

Christ: Yes, they may. Nonetheless, it is true that we can speak now because you can receive my thoughts in your mind and consciousness.

Bob: But really there's nothing special at all about me, so why don't more people do this? Although I don't know that other people don't commune with you. Perhaps they do?

Christ: People commune with me in different ways, but most do not do this consciously, as you are now.

Bob: Maybe then, this somehow belongs to my destiny path? I mean, that I started to communicate with those in spirit some 18 years ago.

Christ: Yes, it does indeed belong to your destiny. You are a student of Rudolf Steiner's Spiritual Science, and this in itself has prepared you for the work that you do now.

Bob: So, you know of Rudolf Steiner?

Christ: Yes, I know of Rudolf Steiner, both in his past incarnation and in his next incarnations. He is a true servant of the Light and the Word of God.

Bob: Do you perhaps know of all people in their incarnations on earth?

Christ: I am in everyone; therefore, nothing is hidden from me.

Bob: According to Rudolf Steiner, we can expect an incarnation of Ahriman imminently. Is this true?

Christ: It is very true. Ahriman must incarnate in order to perform his God-given role in human evolution.

Bob: God allows him to do this?

Christ: It is part of the Divine Plan that Ahriman must make his appearance upon the earth, just as I lived on the earth 2000 or so years ago.

Bob: So, it is inevitable?

Christ: Yes, it is.

Bob: And what should we do about this, about him?

Christ: You should learn to recognize him, so that you are not deceived by the lies he will tell you. You must learn to see the truth, from the deception that he will bring.

Bob: In a time when we speak of 'fake news 'and conspiracy theories, it may not be so easy to discern the truth from the falsehoods?

Christ: You must find the truth within you, and then you will also perceive the truth around you.

Bob: And the truth will set us free?

Christ: Yes, the truth will set you free, as the 'Comforter' that I have sent unto you.

Bob: The Holy Spirit?

Christ: Yes, the Holy Spirit, which is also the Christ within, which is I AM.

Bob: I am wondering what else I should ask. Are you with us both in life on earth and in our lives after death?

Christ: I am always with you, but you do not always see me.

Bob: How do you mean, O Christ?

Christ: Those who have died and do not realize that they are in Spirit may be shrouded in darkness. Only when they see the light will they also then see me.

Bob: I believe that when we are on earth, we can help those who have died by remembering them and giving them spiritual food, nourishment. Is that correct?

Christ: You can indeed, my son. By offering spiritual food to those in Spirit, you can help them find their way to the light.

Bob: So, this points to a real working together, a real conscious cooperation between the so-called living and the so-called dead?

Christ: Yes, it does, and it is something that should be cultivated more and more. Love is the key that unites all humanity, and through love I will also be present to all who seek me.

Bob: I feel that what you are saying, O Christ, has also to do with our inner freedom?

Christ: Yes, freedom and love belong together, and I must respect this in every human being.

Bob: Are you not love, O Christ?

Christ: Yes, I am love, and through love I respect human freedom.

Bob: I think that on this note I will bring our conversation to a close for now. Is that all right?

Christ: It is always all right. I will respond when you ask me to. Ask and you will receive. God's blessing be with you, and my peace, my son.

Bob: Thank you so much.

*

Note: As I said at the start, I do feel quite unworthy to speak to the Christ Being. Rudolf Steiner says that he is 'the greatest being who has trodden upon the earth'. How can we speak with such a profound spiritual being? The answer must be, in our own hearts, in sincerity and earnestness. Because, 'Deep in each human soul, Being of Christ indwells'. This must be the mystery to which St Paul pointed when he said, 'Not I, but Christ in me'. What became a reality for Paul can become, it seems, a reality for each of us also.

*

After the above was written, my friend Michael asked me if I would ask more about the nature of the Holy Spirit. Therefore, I had a further session where I posed the following questions to Christ

Bob: O Christ, may I ask you a further question?

Christ: Yes, my son, you can.

Bob: Can you tell me more about the Holy Spirit? How should we imagine, or see, his influence today?

Christ: The Holy Spirit is the Comforter, the Spirit of Truth, who was sent out from the Father through me. This Holy Spirit, like the Father and myself, lives in each person. This is the 'Spirit of Truth', who was sent out from the Father through me. This Holy Spirit, like the Father and myself, lives in each person. This is the Spirit of Truth and it is also me, myself. The Holy Spirit and I are one, just as we are one with the Father. So, seek the Holy Spirit within yourselves, where you find me also.

Bob: I think I've read somewhere, probably in Steiner's writings, that the Holy Spirit is the transformed, or redeemed, Lucifer. Is this true, O Christ?

Christ: Yes, this is also true. Lucifer is also a brother to me and therefore we belong together on a higher level of being.

Bob: Even though he is also described as an adversarial spirit for humanity?

Christ: There are different ways of looking at Lucifer. On the highest level, he and I are at one.

Bob: Does he not oppose you, O Christ?

Christ: No, he does not oppose me, but he does have a role to fulfil for humanity.

Bob: So, Lucifer has then something to do with the Holy Spirit?

Christ: Yes, in his deepest being he does.

137

Bob: So, I'm getting the impression that things are not just black and white, so to speak. Rather, they need to be looked at on different levels of being. Is that correct, O Christ?

Christ: It is indeed. What is necessary for human development is not the same as what is needed on the higher levels of being.

Bob: Thank you. Have I received your words aright, O Christ? I'm concerned that I do not misrepresent what I think you are saying.

Christ: You are receiving my words, my thoughts, correctly, yes.

Bob: Well then, thank you again.

Christ: May God's grace be with you, and my peace.

*

After the preceding dialogue, I decided to find out more of what Steiner had said about the Holy Ghost. I found the following on page 171 of the book *Paths of the Christian Mysteries** by Virginia Sease and Manfred Schmidt-Brabant:

> Rudolf Steiner says that this Count of St Germain possesses a copy of a document buried deep in the archives of the Vatican. This document contains the secret that the Holy Spirit is to be born in human beings and that this Holy Spirit is in fact Lucifer, risen again in new glory. The human being permeated by the Christ begins to redeem Lucifer when – permeated by him – he understands the Christ through the wisdom of Lucifer. Lucifer streams through the human being and arises as the Holy Spirit.

I was pleased to have found this, as it seems to confirm everything that was said by Christ in the dialogue above.

---

* Temple Lodge Publishing, 2003.

Eighth Conversation

Prologue

I realize that for me to claim to have had conversations with Christ will seem to many people beyond belief. Yes, people may try to be understanding towards me, perhaps recognizing that the author seems to be sincere and serious. However, he must nevertheless be misguided, or at best mistaking one of his alleged spirit guides for the living Christ Being. Well, I can sympathise with this viewpoint, but I know my spirit guides sufficiently well not to confuse them with the one to whom I'm speaking in these pages.

On the other hand, I'm not trying as such to convince anyone that I am speaking with Christ, and certainly not against any reader's best judgement. No, I am more than content to let each person who chooses to read this book make up their own mind.

However, I will repeat what I said before. If Christ really does live within each of us, deep down in our own soul, why should we not speak with him? If he is a part of us, indeed the best part of us, as our true humanity, then doesn't it make sense to try to tune in with him?

Yes, I will agree that if Christ was some remote God, living in some other part of the universe or up in heaven, then maybe we should rather communicate with those closer to us; perhaps our spirit guides, or even a personal guardian angel. Indeed, I would certainly advocate speaking with these very beings, who are connected to us. But according to Christ himself, he is also closely aligned with each of us. In fact, if he does really dwell within us, then he couldn't be closer than he is! Therefore, amazing though it is to imagine that we can learn to speak directly with Christ, I have to reiterate, then why not?

Even if someone concedes to this line of thought, they might still say, 'But what you report as such conversations might be inaccurate. You might have somehow put your own words into his mouth, so to speak, and therefore, quite inadvertently deceived yourself. You didn't mean to, but nonetheless you probably have'. Well, who knows, you may be right, but I actually don't think you are. Why? Because I have received these words, these thoughts, telepathically in exactly the same way as I have done over the past 18 years with my guides. For me, it is a tried and tested method, which I have learned to trust. If that were not the case, then I would also have to admit to some form of self-deception. But then my previous published writings with my guides would also be very questionable indeed. However, the whole tone and tenor of these books, and the flow of thoughts that they contain, leads me to believe in their authenticity.

So, suffice it to say that to the best of my knowledge and my intuition, what is now presented in this book also has a genuine basis. Or to put it more simply, I believe it is true communication with that Being who has united himself with us, and that I am indeed conversing with Christ. This evening I will again turn to him and see what we will speak about together.

Conversation

Bob: O Christ, may I turn to you again inwardly and speak with you?

Christ: Yes, my son, you may. Tell me what it is that you wish to know.

Bob: Well, I want to be absolutely honest with my readers. I do not wish in any way to be deceptive. So, let me ask you again, O Christ, how is it possible for me to speak with you?

Christ: It is possible because I am in you and you are in me, and because of this, you have direct access to me, as do all human beings who live on earth.

Bob: And yet I am neither clairvoyant nor an initiate, nor anyone special, I would say.

Christ: No, and you do not need to have any of these gifts, my son. You only need to believe that it is possible to speak with me and then do so.

Bob: So, could anyone do what I am doing?

Christ: Yes, they could if they wished to and are able to listen inwardly to what lives within them in their own hearts and souls.

Bob: Well, perhaps it is my work with my spirit guides that has helped me to learn to put my trust in this way of communing?

Christ: You have worked with those who live in spirit worlds, and you have developed with them your method of doing so.

Bob: And yet you say, O Christ, that others could also do this if they wanted?

Christit: Yes, if they wanted. It lies within their own freedom to learn to do what you have done. But the choice is theirs. I am always ready to respond to those who seek me within themselves.

Bob: Thank you. But just to clarify – we don't need to be highly developed spiritually to speak with you?

Christ: No, you do not, but you do need to believe it is possible. If someone believes it is impossible, then they put a stone in their own path. I do not put that stone there, but they do.

Bob: Let me turn again, O Christ, to ask you about the times in which we are living in the twenty-first century. Is this an important time, I mean in evolutionary terms?

Christ: It is a very important time because it is the time when human beings should start to wake up to their own spirituality, to the core of their being.

Bob: But aren't many very engrossed, and indeed burdened, by material things only?

Christ: They are indeed, and this is a pity, because you can't find yourself in a purely material world. In such a world, you lose yourself rather than find yourself.

Bob: Yes, I have believed for many years that it is necessary to seek a spiritual way of life in order to find our true purpose and meaning. Do you agree, O Christ?

Christ: I do agree, because I know that in the physical world alone, you will never find that meaning and purpose that your soul seeks.

Bob: So, I guess the only question is, how to help bring about a new spiritual awareness worldwide?

Christ: Yes, that awareness is breaking through the veils of materialism, but it needs to be received into human hearts and souls.

Bob: Is the spiritual world and its beings trying to help us to wake up spiritually?

Christ: Yes, the powers that be are doing all they can to stir the souls of human beings into wakefulness. However, all depends on the response of the human beings themselves. The spirit beings cannot trespass on human freedom.

Bob: So, it could be an uphill battle?

Christ: Yes, it could, but of course, here and there souls become awake, more awake, to who they really are.

Bob: I should imagine that the adversarial powers are also doing their best to prevent us waking up?

Christ: They are, indeed. Therefore, it is all the more important that people recognize what forces and powers are trying to influence them in the time in which you live now.

Bob: And how can *you* help us with this situation, O Christ?

Christ: I wait to be called upon. When I am called upon, I can respond, but if I am not called upon, then I have to wait until I am.

Bob: Well, maybe this is difficult when I think of different religions, beliefs, dogmas, teachings, sects, etc. I mean that perhaps peoples' set beliefs can get in the way of a direct, simple approach to you?

Christ: Yes, that is true. Too much dogma, too many set beliefs, can undercut what in all truth should be a simple and direct line to me.

Bob: But of course, many people perhaps would not even think of that possibility?

Christ: Yes, they would not, because their eyes are blinkered, their ears are deaf and their hearts are hardened.

Bob: Which, I feel, is a sad thing to hear, isn't it?

Christ: Yes, it is, but such is the price of freedom. Everyone is free to remain blind, deaf and dumb if they so choose.

Bob: Well, in a very little and very modest way, I hope this book may help to point the way that others may choose to follow.

Christ: Yes, I hope so too, and that is why I am more than happy to speak with you, my son. I know that your heart is in the right place.

Bob: Well, I hope so, though I am only too aware of my shortcomings and imperfections.

Christ: That does not matter. That does not prevent you speaking with me, inwardly. I did not come to lead the faithful only. I came to all men and women, to all people, to help them realize who they really are: the children of God. The sons and daughters of my Father who art in heaven.

Bob: Well, I am now 75 years old and will be 76 next Easter time, and I certainly do need all the help I can get to become a better human being.

Christ: Ask and you will receive. This is true now, and it always has been and always will be.

Bob: Yes, but many people perhaps don't think to ask you?

Christ: Yes, that is true. When they do, I will answer them.

Bob: Even as I sit here with pen in hand and write down the thoughts that I receive, I do find this quite amazing and humbling. Can you understand this?

Christ: Yes, I do understand it, but it should come to pass that more and more people can do what you are doing, my son, and have trust in their own abilities.

Bob: This has been quite a lengthy path for me to walk along.

Christ: Yes, it has, and for each one, each person, the path will be as long as it takes for them to truly believe in themselves, and also in me.

Bob: But the important thing is that everyone can find their path for themselves?

Christ: Yes, they can, as soon as they start to seek for it, and that is also then part of their own awakening to themselves, to who they truly are.

Bob: You know of course, O Christ, that many people struggle with themselves, even hate themselves at times?

Christ: I do indeed, and it saddens me greatly that this is so. I lived on earth, and I know the hearts and minds of men. Therefore, I feel only love and compassion for all people, each one who is given to me.

Bob: So you, O Christ, are truly our helper and guide, the light of our life?

Christ: I am, because the Father has given you all to me, to lead back to his house, his heavenly mansion. His house has many rooms; no one is left homeless who turns to me for help.

Bob: That is certainly very reassuring, is it not?

Christ: It is, and it is true. I only speak what is true in the words that are given me by the Father.

Bob: I think I will draw to a close now. Thank you for speaking with me once again this evening, O Christ.

Christ: Thank you, my son, for allowing me to draw into your heart and your consciousness. May God's blessing be with you, and my peace.

Bob: Thank you.

Ninth Conversation

Prologue

This last conversation will take place on the last of the Holy Nights, 2023, on the evening of 5 January. Of course, these conversations are not limited by such a special holy time as comes with each Christmastide. They surely can take place on any day of the year. But it was just at this Christmas that the thought came to me to do this. It was a new thought, a new inspiration, I might say. I'm very grateful that it came to me, and that, for the first time, I have engaged with the Christ in this conscious way.

*

This morning, 5 January, I watched on the television the funeral of Pope Benedict XVI. It took place in St Peter's Square, Vatican City, Rome. The square was filled with thousands of people, and also many red-cloaked cardinals, all men of course. Pope Francis, himself elderly and infirm, presided over the funeral of his predecessor. It is a unique event that the present pope is there for the emeritus pope, who died on New Year's Eve, this Christmastide. Well, it was quite something to see this occasion being televised as it happened. As well as the cardinals, there were many other priests present, who helped to distribute the consecrated bread as the Requiem Mass took place. A large gathering of the faithful of the Roman Catholic Church, very impressive to see. And yet, it is good to bear in mind, I feel, that in the modern twenty-first century, we do not necessarily need a priest, or even a pope, to be an intermediary between Christ and ourselves. Nor, probably, for God and ourselves. At least, this is my conviction, from the experiences that I have had during this Christmas period. Therefore, Saint Paul's saying, 'Not I, but Christ in me', must surely apply to each one of us when we come towards that inner recognition for ourselves. Having said this, I do not mean to imply that we are then somehow ready-made saints! Only that if we look within, we can also find the Christ alive in our own souls, however unworthy we may feel about that fact.

Now it is evening, I have spent some time listening to music, whilst being illumined by the shining lights on our Christmas tree. I will let the words of meditation pass through my mind in order to enter into the appropriate mood of soul for another conversation.

Conversation

Bob: O Christ, may I speak with you once again this evening?

Christ: Yes, my son, you can speak with me. Tell me what it is you wish to know.

Bob: Can you tell me how we should understand the words of St Paul, 'Not I, but Christ in me'?

Christ: These words are to be understood quite literally. As I live in you, so you may also feel identified with me in your deepest being. Therefore, your 'I' can be my 'I'.

Bob: And would that mean a great change in our everyday personality?

Christ: No, this need not be the case. Your everyday personality is one thing, but your deepest soul-life is another. It is in the depth of your soul that you will find me alive.

Bob: So, we don't need to become like saints in order to come to an experience of you, O Christ?

Christ: No, you do not.

Bob: Well, that is just as well, I think, because for most of us that would be far too great a task!

Christ: Yes, but remember it is the Church that confers sainthood, not myself.

Bob: Do you mean that even as quite ordinary people, shall I say, we can draw near to you inwardly?

Christ: Yes, that is correct. I am there for every human soul, however that soul may be seen in the eyes of the Church, or any other institution, for that matter.

Bob: Are you actually our 'higher self', as it is called? I could also say, our true, spiritual being?

Christ: I am one with your higher self, with your true, spiritual being. Your being and I form a oneness.

Bob: And how is that, then, with our guardian angel? Is this being also one with our higher self?

Christ: No, the angel is a separate being, but points the way towards recognizing your own higher self.

Bob: And what is your relationship, O Christ, to each person's guardian angel?

Christ: I am also the leader for your guardian angel. I am the one who enables the angel to guide you on your path of destiny, towards your own karmic aims and goals.

Bob: So, our angels can look to you, O Christ, for their help and guidance?

Christ: Yes, they can. I am there for the angels, as I am there for each of you.

Bob: Who is the Father, your Father?

Christ: He is the Alpha and the Omega, the beginning and the end of all things. He is the one who has created the universe.

Bob: And were you then with him also at the beginning of all things?

Christ: Yes, I was. The Father and I are one. What the Father does, I do also.

Bob: And how is that with Jesus of Nazareth, in whom you incarnated – as I understand it – when he was 30 years old?

Christ: Jesus of Nazareth is a Master and a leader of mankind. He lives on earth again and again, and is a great helper to mankind.

Bob: I feel I am treading on holy ground with such questions. So, let me ask something different. Considering the troubles that we have on earth, largely if not completely man-made, do we have a future?

Christ: You do indeed have a future, because I have united myself with you. It is through me that the future of the earth and the future of mankind has been secured.

Bob: Yes, Rudolf Steiner in his anthroposophy says as much, I believe. He says that the Mystery of Golgotha, your deeds at Easter, have given the whole evolution of humanity its very meaning and purpose.

Christ: Yes, that is correct. Through me, humanity will be allowed to fulfil its God-given destiny.

Bob: But if you hadn't intervened, O Christ, would our future have been jeopardized by the adversary powers?

Christ: Yes, it would have been. But God would not allow this to take place, and therefore I came to the earth to redeem it.

Bob: As I understand it, in the Gospels your teaching is one of love. 'Love your neighbour as yourself'. Anyone can understand it, I would say.

And yet, as human beings, we still seem very far from putting this teaching into practice.

Christ: Yes, this is true, but 2,000 years is not a long time in the history of the world. It will still take thousands of years for this teaching to become a reality in all human souls.

Bob: But why is it so difficult for us to practise this love, this unconditional love?

Christ: Because it is unconditional. Love, as usually understood or felt, is conditional. It expects something in return. True love expects nothing whatsoever, and this is why it takes a long time for human beings to learn this, to do this.

Bob: And together with this, of course, we have freedom. Or rather, freedom is an ideal that we continue to aspire towards.

Christ: Yes, it is, my son. It is the great aim of evolution that all human beings will become inwardly free beings. But, like love, this takes time and lifetimes to realize.

Bob: The goal of our earth evolution for humanity is love and freedom?

Christ: It is. This is the God-given goal which is set before you all.

Bob: And is this something unique to the human race, or do the beings in spirit worlds already have love and freedom?

Christ: They know love and devotion for the Father, for their God, but freedom, such as human beings can acquire it, is uniquely human.

Bob: So, are you saying, O Christ, that spirit beings, the so-called spiritual hierarchies, are unfree?

Christ: When freedom is understood in the human sense, then yes, they are unfree.

Bob: Do we then have a unique role to play in the universe, in the cosmos?

Christ: Yes, you do. Through you, other beings can also acquire their freedom.

Bob: I don't understand how that can be.

Christ: It is the gift of humanity to the cosmos.

Bob: This is very difficult for me to grasp, considering that there are, as I understand it, many ranks of spiritual beings in the cosmos. Some of whom, like the Seraphim and Cherubim, are close to the throne of God, so to speak?

Christ: Yes, this is also true, my son. All will be revealed in time.

Bob: From what you say, it does sound that humanity's role is much more significant than our modern scientists and astronomers imagine?

Christ: It is quite different than they imagine it to be.

Bob: Clearly, there are important questions to be asked. Indeed, I have already asked some of these. But truth be told, it may be, or rather is, beyond our understanding to grasp all of this, I feel.

Christ: All things will be revealed in time and beyond time. There is enough for human beings to work at now without knowing all the answers. There is much to put right in the world as it is, do you not agree?

Bob: I certainly do agree. But with God's help and yours, O Christ, we stand a chance of moving ahead.

Christ: With us, you do. Therefore, God's blessing and my peace be with you.

Bob: I thank you.

Note: With this, I feel that this ninth conversation has come to a natural end. There is only a certain point where asking questions is still meaningful, considering my inability to grasp the full significance of the answers. After all, we, or I, am inclined towards abstractions, whereas the reality has to be experienced and lived. But, 'with God, all things are possible'.

Conclusion to Part III

When I wrote the Introduction to Part III, I did not yet know if I would be able to have telepathic conversations with Christ. I hoped this would be the case, but I did not know. However, when I sat down the first evening and put this question to him, I received an immediate, positive response. On that basis, the nine conversations contained here flowed onto the pages. I offer them here to you, as reader, to consider, to contemplate, to think upon... I leave you entirely free to accept, reject or perhaps, best of all, to keep an open mind on all these things – to see if what you have read somehow resonates with you, within you. Above all, does it give you cause to think about the possibility that the Christ can reveal himself to each of us in our modern times? If so, then we don't need to rely on history, if indeed there are any truly reliable historical records of his life on earth, now more than 2,000 years ago. We don't even have to put our trust or faith in the four Gospel accounts, though if we want to, that's of course fine. But what I'm trying to point to is that the Christ – as our guide, comforter and saviour – is available and accessible today, within our *own* experiences. We only need to be open to his presence, his actuality.

Now, in saying this, please don't misunderstand me. I'm not a Gospel evangelist! I'm not wishing to stir up any fervent emotions or ecstasy, or anything like that. No, I'm just asking that we seriously consider that Christ is indeed alive and well today, and that he will make – does make – himself available to us.

In the first conversation with Christ, I wrote the following:

Bob: Well, I would indeed ask you to show yourself in whatever way that you can, before I finish the conversations that I have with you.
Christ: This I will do. Be alert and awake, and I will show myself to you. Perhaps when you least expect it.

As I write this Conclusion however, on the morning of 6 January, I cannot claim to have seen the Etheric Christ – or if I have, I am not aware of it. However, I did have a new thought, which came strongly to me when I went shopping this morning. I thought that, if I am open to it, I will be able to perceive the Christ *in the other person*, in those that I meet in the course of my ordinary life. If it *is* true that Christ lives deep in every human soul, then I can seek to find him in my neighbour, even if that person is a stranger to me. This is a powerful thought, which reverberates within me. Could this thought be Christ's response to my request that he would show himself to me? This particular thought struck me on this first day of Epiphany in the Christian year. It gives me a warm feeling. Is this what also inspired and motivated Mother Theresa of Calcutta, in her work with the down-and-outs in India? Did she not say that she saw Christ in everyone? Now that this thought has entered into me, after I have recorded the nine conversations in this book, I think that it may begin to take root: that I begin to look for, to seek, the Christ in *you*. But, let me now not get beyond myself! It's not something to shout out loud, but rather something to think of again and again. Let's leave it at that, shall we? Thank you for letting me share this experience with you.

Now, the holy Christmastime draws to a close for this year. In our sitting room, we have our Christmas tree. There will be a big hole in that space when I take the tree out! There always is. But I am grateful that it has been possible to look upon that symbol, that sign of hope, since I put it on its stand and brought it into the house a few days before Christmas Eve. Our tree, like the many Christmas trees I experienced in my 40 years in a Camphill Community, has special decorations. On its branches are 30 red (paper) roses, and three white ones near the top. They stand for the 30 years of the life of Jesus of Nazareth and the three years of the life of Christ in Jesus, from the baptism by John in the River Jordan to the cross on Golgotha. Near the base of the tree, on the lowest branches, hang apples. They are a symbol, a reminder, of the Tree of Knowledge in the Garden of Eden, in Paradise, which Adam and Eve ate from – the one tree that God had forbidden them to eat the fruits thereof. Well, they did it nonetheless (apparently), and so had to leave Paradise and find their feet upon the earth, just like the rest of us.

And then we also find certain planetary signs on the Christmas tree. The symbols for Saturn, Sun, Moon, Mars and Mercury, Jupiter and Venus. These represent the path of evolution that Rudolf Steiner described in his anthroposophical teachings, in which he spoke of the incarnations of our earth, both past and future. Not only we as individuals reincarnate but, according to Steiner, the whole planet undergoes such transformations.

At the very top of the tree is the five-pointed star or pentagram, said to be the cosmic symbol of man. 'Man' in the sense of a fulfilled humanity, a humanity that has achieved its God-given goal of realizing love and freedom. Not surprising, then, that we have to look to the very top of the tree!

There are also other things on the tree, but I leave those for now. There is just one thing more. Under the tree, in Camphill, were located the carved wooden figures representing Mother Mary, Joseph and the Holy Child. Yes, the shepherds, too, I think, perhaps joined by the kings at Epiphany. This reminds us that, through Jesus, the Christ came to earth, to walk on the same ground that we also tread, to become the 'Son of Man'.

Dear friends, let me finish this book by quoting once again the meditation verse that I included in the Introduction to Part III.

In the beginning was Christ,
And Christ was with the Gods,
And a God was Christ.
Deep in each human soul
Being of Christ indwells.
In my soul too He dwells
And He will lead me
To the true meaning of my life.

I received this verse from a concerned and caring friend some 50 years ago, when I was a student at Emerson College. I still have the copy that she (Olive Whicher) gave me, in her own handwriting. I begin now to work with this content, and to see if I can make it my own; that it may reveal itself to me.

All blessings, Bob

Afterword

In April 1986, John McCarthy, a journalist, was kidnapped in Beirut and held captive for over five years. In *Some other Rainbow* he describes an experience he had in the early phase of this time:

> I was in solitary for three months but after two months, with not the slightest hint that I might be released, I got more frightened. So many of my reflections had left me feeling inadequate that I really began to doubt that I could cope alone and one morning these fears became unbearable. I stood in the cell sinking into despair. I felt that I was literally sinking, being sucked down into a whirlpool. I was on my knees, gasping for air, drowning in hopelessness and helplessness. I thought that I was passing out. I could only think of one thing to say – 'Help me please, oh God, help me.' The next instant I was standing up, surrounded by a warm bright light. I was dancing, full of joy. In the space of a minute, despair had vanished, replaced by boundless optimism.
>
> What had happened? I had never had any great faith, despite a Church of England upbringing. But I felt I had to give thanks, but to what? Unsure of the nature of the experience, I felt most comfortable acknowledging the Good Spirit which seemed to have rescued me. It gave me great strength to carry on and, more importantly, a huge renewal of hope – I was going to survive. Throughout my captivity, I would take comfort from this experience, drawing on it whenever optimism and determination flagged.*

In 1911, Rudolf Steiner (1861–1925), who introduced anthroposophy and spiritual science to humanity, remarked in a lecture:

> Many will have experiences when sitting silently in their room, heavy-hearted and oppressed, not knowing which way to turn. The door will open and the etheric Christ will appear

---

* *Some other Rainbow*, John McCarthy and Jill Morrell, Corgi Books (1993).

and speak words of consolation. Christ will become a living comforter and in the future this will happen for a considerable number of people.*

There is an expectation in some Christian confessions that Christ will reappear in human form and be with us on the earth to be our comforter once again. So far, this expectation has not been fulfilled, as far as I know, but what has happened is that such experiences as described by John McCarthy have happened to others, myself included, though not in such dramatic circumstances. Unless they are spoken about, we will not know that such events have and are taking place. Presumably, they are of a nature which the recipient would not shout about 'from the house tops', only being grateful they have been saved from 'drowning in hopelessness and helplessness'.

Thus, it can be considered that Christ is present in the world, among human beings, in times of need, though not as previously, two thousand years ago. My understanding is that it is this being that Bob Woodward is conversing with here.

To the mind of a materialist, who cannot countenance the existence of a world of spiritual reality present alongside and interpenetrating earthly life beyond the physical plane, the existence of spirit guides and the Christ will most likely make no sense.

However, I believe that today we human beings live in a world which is slowly moving forward, beyond the iron necessity for physical material proof of 'things', to include proof through experience. Due to this change, it is necessary to be tolerant, open-minded and understanding towards the experiences others share, even if at first hearing they appear unbelievable.

The above calls for an extended capacity and quality of listening, and in this book we are able to read and listen to the world out of which the Good Spirit came to John McCarthy, and may come to others in times of need.

In these conversations between Bob and Christ, which the reader can countenance or not, my main impression is that this being – *Christ* – is not only the teacher and healer of two thousand years ago, but a potential advisor and guide to human beings who have to learn through

---

* *The Etherisation of the Blood*, lecture by Rudolf Steiner given in Basle, Switzerland on 1 October 1911.

experience – good and not so good. We have to come to our own insights through conscience and freedom – not through organized religion, as in the past and often still today. The predominance of the outer sense world is added to by the reality of inner experience, but this transition will take time, learning and listening, and in this world of spirit there are only beings, as Rudolf Steiner has explained.

Thus, these conversations open a door to a relationship to the being of Christ, and what his hopes are for we human beings. Bob is not expecting the reader to believe in what lies beyond this door, a door opened by questions and listening, but offers accounts of particularly intimate and tentative conversations not often shared. It takes some trust and courage to do this – to open the door. Thank you, Bob, for turning the handle!

Michael Luxford

Further Reading

Part I:

Cook, G. (1985) *The New Mediumship*, The White Eagle Publishing Trust

Greaves, H. (1969) *Testimony of Light*, World Fellowship Press Ltd

Pogacnik, Ana (2022) *Being Human in the Now–Conversations with the Soul of My Sister*, Interactions

Ratsey, I. (1966) *Pioneering in Conscious and Cooperative Mediumship*, Regency Press

Steiner, R. (1995) *Intuitive Thinking as a Spiritual Path*, SteinerBooks

Steiner, R. (1999) *Staying Connected – How to Continue Your Relationships with Those who Have Died*, Anthroposophic Press

Van Praagh, J. (2017) *Wisdom From Your Spirit Guides*, Hay House

Wetzl, R. (1974) *The Bridge Over the River*, SteinerBooks

White, R. (2004) *Working with Spirit Guides*, Piatkus

White, R. & Swainson, M. (1971) *Gildas Communicates*, Neville Spearman

Woodward, B. (2007) *Spirit Communications*, Athena Press

Woodward, B. (2018) *Trusting in Spirit – The Challenge*, AuthorHouse

Woodward, B. (2020) *Knowledge of Spirit Worlds and Life after Death*, Clairview Books

Woodward, B. (2022) *Journeying into Spirit Worlds, Safely and Consciously*, Clairview Books

Woodward, B. (2022) *Karma in Human Life*, Clairview Books

Part II:

Ackroyd, P. (1999) *Blake*, Vintage Books

Byrne, L. (2008) *Angels in My Hair*, Arrow Books

Byrne, L. (2011) *Stairways to Heaven*, Coronet

Byrne, L. (2013) *A Message of Hope from the Angels*, Coronet

Byrne, L. (2015) *Love from Heaven*, Coronet

Byrne, L. (2018) *Angels at My Fingertips*, Coronet

Carmichael, A. (1966) *The Sun Dances*, Christian Community Press

Hodson, G. (1988) *The Brotherhood of Angels and Men*, Theosophical Publishing House

Raven, H. (2009) *The Angel Bible*, Godsfield Press

Steiner, R. (1996) *Angels*, Rudolf Steiner Press

Steiner, R. (2000) *Guardian Angels*, Rudolf Steiner Press

Steiner, R. (2003) *The Reappearance of Christ in the Etheric*, SteinerBooks

White, R. (1997) *Working with Your Guides and Angels*, Samuel Weiser Inc.

Woodward, B. (2007) *Spirit Communications*, Athena Press

Woodward, B. (2018) *Trusting in Spirit – The Challenge*, Author House

Woodward, B. (2020) *Knowledge of Spirit Worlds and Life after Death*, Clairview Books

Woodward, B. (2022) *Journeying into Spirit Worlds*, Clairview Books

Woodward, B. (2022) *Karma in Human Life*, Clairview Books

Part III:

(Dr Rudolf Steiner referred to the Christ in very many of his lectures and books. Below is a small selection of these.)

Steiner, R. (1972) *Verses and Meditations*, Rudolf Steiner Press

Steiner, R. (1973) *From Jesus to Christ*, Rudolf Steiner Press

Steiner, R. (1976) *The Christ Impulse and the Development of Ego-consciousness*, SteinerBooks

Steiner, R. (1981) *The Festivals and Their Meaning*, Rudolf Steiner Press

Steiner, R. (1984) *How Can Mankind Find the Christ Again?*, SteinerBooks

Steiner, R. (1997) *An Outline of Esoteric Science*, SteinerBooks

Woodward, B. (2007) *Spirit Communications*, Athena Press

Woodward, B. (2018) *Trusting in Spirit – The Challenge*, Author House

Woodward, B. (2020) *Knowledge of Spirit Worlds and Life after Death*, Clairview Books

Woodward, B. (2022) *Karma in Human Life*, Clairview Books

More About the Author

I was born in 1947 in the UK. At the age of 11, I had the good fortune to fail my 11+ exam, which was then the entrance into state secondary education. Through this stroke of destiny, I entered Wynstones, an independent Rudolf Steiner School in Gloucestershire, where I remained for seven years until I was 18. Following A-levels in maths and physics, I went to university, and a year later, became a university dropout!

At the age of 23, at Easter 1970, I was guided to become a co-worker at the Sheiling School in Thornbury, a centre of the Camphill Community based on the teachings of Rudolf Steiner (1861–1925). Apart from a year at Emerson College in Sussex, I spent some 40 years within the Camphill Movement, living with and teaching children with special educational needs. I retired from this work in 2012.

I became a student of Steiner's anthroposophy having first read one of his fundamental books, *Knowledge of the Higher Worlds, How is it Achieved?*, when I was around 18 years old, now more than 50 years ago. Later, I also became a member of the Anthroposophical Society in Great Britain. I have, however, always tried to keep an open mind, and I consider myself a perpetual student. When I was 46, I received an MEd degree from Bristol University and this was followed by an MPhil when I was 50. In 2011, I was awarded a PhD from the University of the West of England, when nearly 64.

As well as being a qualified curative educator, I am also a spiritual healer and an author. I took a special interest in understanding autism in children and young people.

I have a lifelong interest in philosophy and spirituality, and in exploring the existential questions of life and death, meaning and freedom. Fundamentally, I see myself as a researcher in the field of spirituality, particularly in my conscious relationships with my spirit guides over the past 19 years and my ongoing work with them.

In 2024, I will have been married for 46 years to my wife, Silke. We have five grown-up children and, currently, ten lively grandchildren. I enjoy walking, swimming, reading, writing, painting and tai chi. My wife and I particularly look forward to our holidays in the beautiful Isles of Scilly in Cornwall. I feel that I have received clear guidance in my own life, and am very grateful for this.

Books to challenge **C** *your perception of reality*

A message from Clairview

We are an independent publishing company with a focus on cutting-edge, non-fiction books. Our innovative list covers current affairs and politics, health, the arts, history, science and spirituality. But regardless of subject, our books have a common link: they all question conventional thinking, dogmas and received wisdom.

Despite being a small company, our list features some big names, such as Booker Prize winner Ben Okri, literary giant Gore Vidal, world leader Mikhail Gorbachev, modern artist Joseph Beuys and natural childbirth pioneer Michel Odent.

So, check out our full catalogue online at
www.clairviewbooks.com
and join our emailing list for news on new titles.

office@clairviewbooks.com

CLAIRVIEW